THE ELECTRONIC HEALTH RECORD REVOLUTION

UNLOCKING HEALTHCARE'S DIGITAL POTENTIAL

THE ELECTRONIC HEALTH RECORD REVOLUTION

UNLOCKING HEALTHCARE'S DIGITAL POTENTIAL

SRINIVASA P. CHAGANTI

™ **PharmaMed Press**
An imprint of BSP Books Pvt. Ltd.
4-4-309/316, Giriraj Lane,
Sultan Bazar, Hyderabad - 500 001.

The Electronic Health Record Revolution:
Unlocking Healthcare's Digital Potential
by Srinivas P. Chaganti

Published by

™ **PharmaMed Press**
An imprint of BSP Books Pvt. Ltd.
4-4-309/316, Giriraj Lane, Sultan Bazar, Hyderabad - 500 001.
Phone: 040-23445688
E-mail: info@pharmamedpress.net
www.bspbooks.net/www.pharmamedpress.net

ISBN: 978-93-49562-65-3 (Hardback)

Preface

Unleashing the Power of Precision in Healthcare

The healthcare landscape is undergoing a fundamental transformation. The era of one-size-fits-all medicine is rapidly giving way to a data-driven paradigm that prioritizes personalized care and targeted interventions. At the heart of this revolution stands a powerful enabler: the Electronic Health Record (EHR).

My own journey into this world was shaped in part by leading the implementation of *IllumiCare*, a smart ribbon technology from the Texas Hospital Association. Inspired by its success at Houston Methodist Hospital, where it was shown to seamlessly overlay real-time, contextual cost and risk data inside the EHR. I saw firsthand how interoperability could move beyond theory to change everyday clinical practice.

This project revealed the hidden drivers of medication costs and resource use. By simply providing transparent data at the point of prescribing, it empowered providers and caregivers to make cost-effective decisions and compare themselves to best practices, all while protecting patient privacy and data security. The experience opened my eyes to the vast, often overlooked, potential of interoperable solutions to transform not just workflows but healthcare outcomes as well.

This book explores the transformative potential of EHRs for both patient care and the evolving ways the pharmaceutical industry engages with clinicians and patients. We will examine the intricate architecture of EHR systems and unveil the wealth of patient data they contain. We'll navigate the complex ethical considerations and regulatory frameworks surrounding data privacy. Most importantly, we'll reveal how EHRs can be a strategic asset in an increasingly digital healthcare ecosystem.

For those working in the pharmaceutical field, EHRs represent an unprecedented opportunity to engage with healthcare providers and patients on a deeper, more meaningful level. By leveraging the real-world data captured in EHRs, companies can gain invaluable insights into patient demographics, treatment patterns, and unmet medical needs. This knowledge empowers the development of targeted strategies that resonate with specific patient populations and address genuine clinical challenges.

However, this newfound capability comes with significant responsibility. We will explore the ethical dimensions of utilizing patient data, ensuring regulatory compliance, and maintaining unwavering respect for patient privacy. The goal is not merely to capitalize on a new channel of engagement but to create value for all stakeholders in the healthcare system.

This book serves as your comprehensive guide to navigating this exciting frontier. Whether you are a veteran in the pharmaceutical industry or new to this field, these pages will equip you with the knowledge and strategies to leverage EHRs effectively. We provide a systematic action plan—from setting data-driven objectives to crafting targeted initiatives and measuring impact.

Ultimately, this book aims to bridge the traditionally separate worlds of patient care and the pharmaceutical industry's collaboration with clinicians and patients. EHRs and interoperable data solutions have the power to reduce waste, improve outcomes, and elevate the patient experience. By harnessing these tools responsibly and ethically, we can create a future where these efforts actively support, rather than merely coexist with, the delivery of optimal patient care.

— Srinivas P Chaganti

Acknowledgements

I am deeply grateful to the many people who have shaped, supported, and inspired this journey.

First and foremost, my heartfelt thanks to my parents, Mr. Subba Rao Chaganti and Mrs. Mahalakshmi—your values and belief in me have been the foundation of all I do.

To my wife, Geetha—thank you for your quiet strength, patience, and unwavering support. To our daughter, Eesha—you are my guiding light, and the reason I strive to be better every day.

To my sisters, Lavanya and Soumya, and your families—Dr. Aditya, Aditi, Surya, TC, and Shriya—thank you for being a steady source of love, laughter, and encouragement. You remind me of the joy in togetherness.

To my in-laws, Mr. Suresh Jotawar and Mrs. Meghamalini, thank you for your kindness and support. And to Geetha's brother and sister-in-law, Dr. Ravikiran and Dr. Latha, and their son Abhinav—your presence has always been generous and grounding.

To my teachers in Hyderabad and Bangalore, thank you for building the foundation of my learning.

To my friends—you know who you are—thank you for your loyalty, humor, and keeping it real.

To my mentors, colleagues, and friends at DHR Health—your commitment to excellence and community care has been a daily source of inspiration.

This book is shaped by the collective wisdom and kindness I have been fortunate to receive. Thank you all for walking this journey with me.

Contents

List of Case Studies

List of Figures

PART ONE: DEMYSTIFYING ELETRONIC HEALTH RECORDS (EHRs)

Part One

Demystifying Electronic Health Records (EHRs)

This section will explore the multifaceted world of Electronic Health Records (EHRs), unpacking their complexity and significance in modern healthcare. We'll examine:

- **The Fundamentals of EHRs**: What exactly are EHRs, and how did they evolve from rudimentary paper charts to the sophisticated digital systems deployed today?
- **The Power Within**: We'll dissect the core components of EHR systems and reveal the extraordinary wealth of patient data they capture: from demographic information and medical histories to treatment outcomes and provider interactions.
- **Navigating the Ecosystem**: This section will map the diverse landscape of EHR platforms, how they communicate, and the persistent challenges and emerging opportunities in health information exchange.
- **Privacy and Security**: As we examine patient data, we will address the critical concerns surrounding privacy and security, exploring regulatory frameworks and industry best practices for safeguarding sensitive health information.

By concluding Part 1, you will comprehensively understand EHRs, their functionalities, and their pivotal role in the healthcare ecosystem. This knowledge will provide the foundation for understanding how EHRs can be leveraged to enhance patient care and pharmaceutical marketing strategies.

Chapter One

The EHR Revolution – Unlocking the Power of Digital Health Records

A Healthcare System at a Crossroads

For decades, patient records were imprisoned in bulging folders, handwritten notes, and overflowing filing cabinets. Healthcare providers struggled daily with missing information, illegible handwriting, and time-consuming retrieval processes. Diagnoses were frequently delayed, and fragmented patient histories compromised critical treatment decisions. The limitations of paper-based systems were most acutely felt in emergencies, where minutes spent waiting for faxed records or searching through charts could mean the difference between life and death.

Adopting Electronic Health Records (EHRs) represents one of modern healthcare's most profound technological revolutions. What began as basic digital versions of paper charts has evolved into sophisticated data ecosystems powered by artificial intelligence, interoperability standards, and predictive analytics. Yet the journey from paper-based documentation to AI-powered clinical decision support has been neither swift nor seamless.

In this chapter, we will explore:

- The evolution of EHRs, from rudimentary handwritten records to sophisticated AI-driven platforms.
- Real-world narratives illustrating the transformative impact of digital health records.
- Case studies and practitioner testimonies demonstrating the tangible benefits of EHR adoption.
- Data-driven insights supported by authoritative research and industry analysis.

The Evolution of EHRs:
From Paper to AI-Powered Intelligence

The transformation of healthcare record-keeping can be traced through three distinct phases:

Era	Characteristics	Challenges
Paper-Based (Pre-1960s)	Handwritten notes, paper charts, manual filing systems	Difficult retrieval, data fragmentation, transcription errors, physical storage limitations
Early Digital Records (1960s–1990s)	Initial adoption of mainframe computers, basic electronic documentation, departmental systems	Prohibitive costs, lack of interoperability, technical limitations, resistance to adoption
EHR Revolution (2000s–Present)	AI-powered decision support, real-time data sharing, interoperability standards, mobile access	Physician burnout, cybersecurity threats, implementation complexities, data governance challenges

FIGURE 1.1: EHR Characteristics.
Source: Office of the National Coordinator for Health IT (ONC), 2021.

Before and After EHR Implementation: Doctors Story

Before EHRs: A Doctor's Daily Struggle

Dr. Rachel Carter, an internal medicine physician at a busy urban hospital, began each day buried under mountains of paperwork. Patient histories were scattered across multiple folders, lab results were frequently missing or misplaced, and routine prescription refills required tedious searches through handwritten notes. She often rushed between departments, attempting to track down critical medical records stored in various physical locations throughout the facility.

Midway through a particularly challenging shift, Dr. Carter treated Mr. Williams, a 65-year-old man admitted with severe chest pain. His prior cardiology tests and medication regimen were unknown, forcing her to order duplicate tests—delaying crucial treatment, increasing costs, and prolonging Mr. Williams' anxiety and discomfort. The situation frustrated both doctor and patient, as repeated diagnostics wasted valuable resources and extended the uncertainty period during a potentially life-threatening event.

By day's end, Dr. Carter spent two additional hours completing paperwork, leaving her physically and mentally exhausted. The time spent manually writing notes and transcribing patient information into different departmental logs meant less time for direct patient care, contributing significantly to her growing sense of professional burnout.

Source: American Medical Association (AMA), Physician Burnout Study, 2020.

After EHRs: A Transformed Workflow

Today, Dr. Carter logs into an AI-integrated EHR system where Mr. Williams' complete medical history appears instantly on her screen. The sophisticated platform automatically retrieves:

- Comprehensive past diagnoses and previous test results from multiple care settings
- A detailed list of current medications, immediately flagging potential drug interactions
- AI-powered clinical alerts warning of subtle patterns suggesting early signs of heart failure.

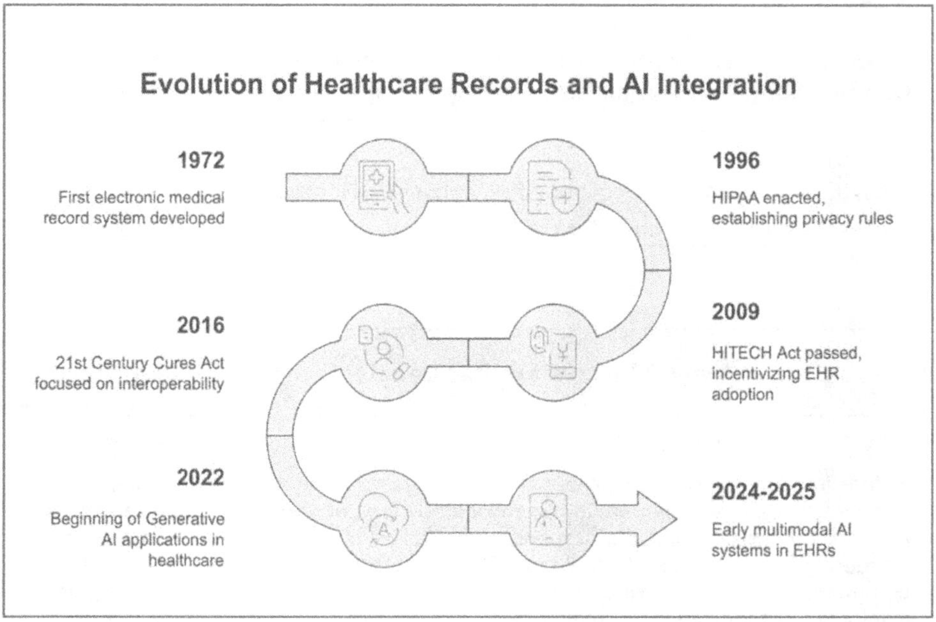

FIGURE 1.2: Evolution of EHRs - A Timeline.

With real-time access to this wealth of clinical data, her decision-making has become faster, safer, and more informed. The new system has dramatically improved collaboration among specialists, as multiple providers can simultaneously review and contribute to the same patient record without the delays and miscommunications that plagued the paper-based era.

Factor	Before EHRs	After EHRs
Efficiency	Time-consuming paperwork, manual chart retrieval, delayed access to information	Instant access to comprehensive patient histories, automated workflows, streamlined documentation
Costs	Higher expenses due to duplicate testing, preventable errors, and administrative burden	Reduced expenditures through efficient data sharing, decreased redundancy, and optimization of clinical resources
Patient Safety	Increased risk of medication errors, incomplete records, and missed diagnoses	Enhanced safety through AI-powered alerts for drug interactions, real-time monitoring, and comprehensive health histories
Care Coordination	Fragmented communication between providers, siloed information, delayed consultations	Seamless information sharing across care teams, integrated specialist notes, and coordinated treatment plans

FIGURE 1.3: Before EHRs and After EHRs - A Comparison.
Source: Harvard T.H. Chan School of Public Health, EHR Impact Study, 2022.

Case Study: Mayo Clinic's Digital Leap – From Chaos to Clarity

Why Change Was Needed

Before implementing a comprehensive EHR system, Mayo Clinic operated within a fragmented data environment that complicated care coordination across its extensive network of facilities and departments. Specialists collaborating on complex cases frequently lacked access to real-time patient information, resulting in inefficiencies, communication gaps, and increased risks of redundant procedures. The distinguished institution recognized that maintaining its reputation for excellence required a fundamental transformation of its information infrastructure.

Contd...

How Mayo Clinic Transformed Its EHR System

Mayo Clinic embarked on an ambitious journey to implement Epic Systems' enterprise-wide EHR, integrating patient data across its entire network of hospitals and clinics. This transformative initiative involved:

- Deploying AI-powered clinical decision support tools to alert physicians of potential complications or adverse events before they occur
- Establishing centralized data repositories ensuring all specialists could access the same comprehensive, up-to-date patient record regardless of location
- Implementing sophisticated predictive analytics capabilities enabling early detection of high-risk conditions and proactive intervention strategies

Results and Impact

- 40% reduction in duplicate testing, translating to millions in cost savings and decreased patient inconvenience (Source: Mayo Clinic Annual Report, 2023)
- 25% improvement in early disease detection rates, leading to significantly better treatment outcomes and reduced complications (Source: New England Journal of Medicine, 2022)
- Dramatic enhancement in care coordination through seamless, real-time data retrieval across previously disconnected departments and facilities (Source: Health Affairs, 2021)

Voices from the Frontline: Healthcare Provider Testimonies

"Before EHRs, coordinating care felt like solving a puzzle with missing pieces. Now, I can instantly access lab results, imaging scans, and specialist notes from anywhere in the hospital. This system hasn't just changed how we document care—it's fundamentally revolutionized how we deliver it." — Dr. Emily Thomas, Cardiologist, New York.

"The reduction in preventable errors alone justifies the transition to digital records. Our hospital has significantly improved patient safety metrics and reduced medication mistakes by over 60%. The ability to automatically cross-check drug interactions and allergies has prevented countless complications that might have gone undetected in a paper-based system." — Dr. Andrew Patel, Chief Medical Officer, Chicago.

Source: American College of Physicians (ACP) Survey, 2022.

Final Thoughts: The Future of EHRs in Healthcare

Today's Electronic Health Records are no longer mere digital replacements for paper charts—they have evolved into intelligent, predictive, and patient-centric platforms driving healthcare innovation. The next frontier in health information technology promises even more transformative capabilities:

- Sophisticated AI-powered diagnostic assistance, enabling truly personalized medicine tailored to individual patient characteristics

- Seamless integration with wearable devices and remote monitoring tools, feeding continuous real-time data into patient records
- Blockchain-based security protocols ensuring safe, patient-controlled data access while maintaining comprehensive audit trails

As we move forward, EHRs will increasingly serve not just as repositories of patient information but as dynamic, interactive platforms that actively contribute to clinical decision-making, research advancement, and healthcare system optimization.

What's Next? In the following chapter, we will explore the core functionalities of modern EHR systems, their key components, and how they contribute to improved patient care and pharmaceutical research. We'll examine the data architecture that makes these systems so powerful and investigate how this wealth of information can be ethically leveraged for both clinical and commercial purposes.

Chapter Two

Navigating the EHR Landscape: Key Components and Functionalities

Electronic Health Records (EHRs) have emerged as the cornerstone of modern healthcare delivery, serving as centralized and secure platforms for managing vast repositories of patient data. But what exactly constitutes an EHR system, and how do its diverse functionalities benefit the various stakeholders across the healthcare ecosystem? This chapter provides a comprehensive exploration of the key components and functionalities that power today's sophisticated EHR systems.

Case Study: A Tale of Two Hospitals: The Cost of Data Silos

Springfield General Hospital (SGH) and Riverview Medical Center (RMC) are two healthcare institutions serving the same metropolitan region. While both implemented EHR systems during the same period, their experiences and outcomes diverged dramatically.

Springfield General Hospital: Struggling with Data Silos

SGH installed an EHR system without prioritizing interoperability. Physicians and staff quickly encountered persistent challenges:

- Patient lab results from external providers remained inaccessible within their system, frequently delaying critical treatment decisions
- Different departments couldn't seamlessly share patient information, forcing nurses to manually input identical patient details across multiple platforms
- Patients expressed growing frustration at having to repeat their medical histories at every appointment, even within the same facility

"It felt like we were drowning in data, but none of it was connected. Instead of helping us, the EHR system actually slowed us down." — Dr. Rebecca Nolan, Chief of Internal Medicine at SGH

Contd...

Riverview Medical Center: A Unified EHR System

In contrast, RMC implemented an interoperable, cloud-based EHR that connected hospitals, specialty clinics, and pharmacies across their network. The results were transformative:

- Reduced duplicate testing cut patient wait times by 30%
- Automated data sharing between departments significantly reduced administrative burden
- Enhanced patient experience as individuals no longer needed to repeatedly provide the same information

This real-world contrast vividly illustrates how EHR adoption without interoperability can exacerbate inefficiencies rather than improving care delivery.

***Key Takeaway*:** Interoperability should be a foundational priority when implementing an EHR system. Selecting the right EHR vendor and ensuring seamless data exchange capabilities can make the critical difference between organizational frustration and operational efficiency.

Demystifying the EHR System

An EHR can be conceptualized as a sophisticated digital filing cabinet with multiple specialized compartments, each dedicated to a specific aspect of a patient's health. Here is a breakdown of the core components typically found within a comprehensive EHR system:

- **Demographics**: This section stores essential patient identification information such as name, date of birth, address, contact information, and emergency contacts.
- **Medical History**: This comprehensive repository details a patient's past and present health conditions, including diagnoses, surgical procedures, immunization records, allergies, and hospitalization events.
- **Medications**: This section maintains a complete inventory of all medications a patient is currently taking, including prescription pharmaceuticals, over-the-counter products, and herbal or nutritional supplements.
- **Clinical Notes**: This component houses detailed progress notes documented by physicians and other healthcare providers during patient

encounters. These notes capture symptoms, diagnoses, treatment strategies, and medication adjustments.

- **Lab Results**: This section stores results from various laboratory tests, including blood panels, urinalysis, and other diagnostic procedures.
- **Imaging Reports**: This component contains images and interpretative reports from diagnostic procedures such as X-rays, CT scans, and MRIs.
- **Social Determinants of Health (SDOH)**: This increasingly important section captures information about non-medical factors that impact a patient's health outcomes, such as housing stability, educational attainment, and social support networks.

Breaking Down the Core Elements of an EHR System

A well-designed EHR system comprises several key components, each fulfilling a crucial role in data management, clinical decision-making, and patient engagement.

EHR Component	Function	Impact on Healthcare
Patient Demographics & Medical History	Stores essential details like allergies, past diagnoses, medications, and lifestyle factors	Enables faster, more informed clinical decision-making
Clinical Decision Support (CDS)	Uses AI algorithms to provide real-time treatment recommendations and alert providers to potential drug interactions	Reduces medication errors and enhances patient safety
Order Entry & Lab Results Integration	Enables electronic prescribing (eRx) and streamlined diagnostic test ordering	Reduces administrative paperwork and improves operational efficiency
Interoperability & Health Information Exchange (HIE)	Ensures seamless data sharing across hospitals, specialists, and pharmacies	Improves continuity of care and reduces redundant testing
Security & Compliance Features	Encrypts patient records to prevent data breaches and ensures HIPAA/GDPR compliance	Protects sensitive patient data from evolving cyber threats

FIGURE 2.1: EHR Components.

Unlocking Functionality: How EHRs Empower Healthcare

Beyond simply storing patient data, modern EHRs offer a diverse range of functionalities that enhance various aspects of healthcare delivery:

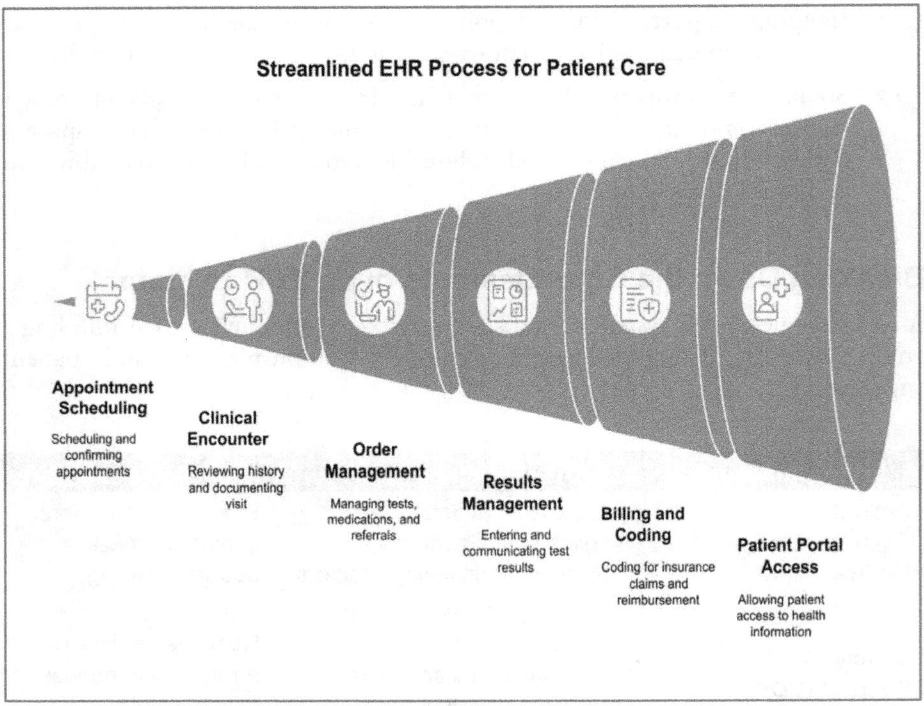

FIGURE 2.2: Streamlined EHR Process for Patient Care.

Clinical Decision Support Systems (CDSS)

These sophisticated built-in tools provide real-time guidance to healthcare providers at the point of care. CDSS can:

- Suggest evidence-based treatment options tailored to a patient's specific medical history and diagnosis
- Automatically flag potential drug interactions and allergies before medication orders are finalized
- Recommend preventive care measures based on individual patient risk factors and population health guidelines

Order Entry and Tracking

EHRs streamline the electronic ordering of medications, laboratory tests, and imaging studies. This systematized approach reduces transcription errors and administrative delays, ensuring orders are received and executed promptly. Additionally, EHRs enable real-time order status tracking, significantly improving communication efficiency across departments and care settings.

Population Health Management

Aggregated EHR data can be analyzed to identify meaningful trends within specific patient populations. This capability empowers healthcare organizations to:

- Target preventive care initiatives toward high-risk population segments
- Develop more effective strategies for managing chronic diseases across communities
- Allocate limited healthcare resources more efficiently based on data-driven population health needs

Quality Improvement and Research

EHR data provides an invaluable resource for healthcare institutions to track performance metrics and identify specific areas for clinical and operational improvement. Additionally, anonymized and aggregated EHR data serves as a rich resource for research initiatives aimed at developing new treatment approaches and improving healthcare outcomes on a broader scale.

Patient Engagement

Many contemporary EHR systems include secure patient portals that allow individuals to access their medical records online. These interfaces empower patients to:

- View laboratory results and diagnostic reports
- Request prescription refills without phone calls
- Schedule appointments with providers
- Track their personal health history over time

Exploring Interoperability: Connecting the Dots

One of the most significant ongoing challenges with EHR implementation is achieving true interoperability—the seamless ability for different EHR systems to communicate and exchange data across organizational boundaries. This limitation becomes particularly problematic when patients receive care from multiple providers utilizing different EHR platforms. Fortunately, substantial advancements are being made to standardize data formats and promote interoperability, facilitating a more unified flow of patient information throughout the healthcare ecosystem.

The Road Ahead: A Future Fueled by Data

As EHR adoption becomes increasingly universal across healthcare settings, we can anticipate further technological advancements in:

Advanced Data Analytics

Leveraging sophisticated big data analytics tools to extract valuable insights from anonymized and aggregated EHR data holds immense potential for enhancing population health management, accelerating clinical research, and enabling truly personalized medicine approaches.

Artificial Intelligence Integration

The integration of artificial intelligence capabilities into EHR systems promises to revolutionize healthcare delivery by automating routine documentation tasks, providing diagnostic assistance, and delivering increasingly sophisticated real-time clinical decision support.

By developing a comprehensive understanding of EHR components and functionalities, we gain deeper appreciation for their transformative potential across the healthcare landscape. This knowledge establishes the foundation for exploring how pharmaceutical companies can ethically leverage EHR data to develop more targeted and effective marketing strategies—the focus of subsequent chapters.

2.1 Data Types Captured in EHR: Demographics, Medical History, Medications, Allergies, and Beyond

Let's explore the comprehensive categories of data captured in modern EHR systems and their significance for patient care:

Demographics: The Foundation of Patient Identification

This fundamental category forms the basis for accurately identifying and tracking individual patients within the healthcare system. It typically includes:

- **Name**: Complete legal name to ensure precise identification, preventing mix-ups with patients having similar names
- **Date of Birth**: Essential for calculating age, a critical factor in determining appropriate preventive screenings and treatment protocols
- **Gender**: May influence certain health risk assessments and treatment approaches
- **Address**: Crucial for appointment reminders, billing purposes, and geographical health trend analysis
- **Phone Number**: Enables direct patient communication regarding appointments, test results, and medication management
- **Emergency Contact Details**: Vital information for urgent situations requiring family notification

Medical History: A Comprehensive Chronicle of Health

This section provides a detailed narrative of a patient's health journey, offering essential context for current health concerns and treatment decisions. It encompasses:

- **Diagnoses**: Documentation of past and present medical conditions (e.g., diabetes, hypertension)
- **Surgeries**: Chronological record of all surgical procedures a patient has undergone
- **Immunizations**: Complete vaccination history with specific dates and formulations
- **Allergies**: Comprehensive list of substances triggering adverse reactions, crucial for preventing potentially life-threatening events
- **Hospitalizations**: Detailed information about past inpatient stays and the clinical reasons for admission
- **Procedures**: Records of all medical procedures performed outside of hospitalization
- **Family History**: Documentation of health conditions present in close relatives that may indicate inherited risk factors

Medications: A Critical Inventory for Safe and Effective Care

This section meticulously tracks all pharmacological agents a patient is taking, including:

- **Prescription Medications**: All provider-prescribed medications with precise dosage, frequency, and duration details
- **Over-the-Counter Drugs**: Non-prescription medications the patient uses regularly or occasionally
- **Herbal Supplements**: Any complementary or alternative preparations the patient incorporates into their health regimen

Vital Signs: Monitoring Essential Physiological Functions

This category captures key physiological measurements providing insights into a patient's current health status:

- **Blood Pressure**: A vital indicator of cardiovascular health and treatment efficacy
- **Body Temperature**: Elevated readings can signal infection or inflammatory processes
- **Heart Rate**: Cardiac rhythm and rate provide important clues about cardiovascular function
- **Respiratory Rate**: The frequency and quality of breathing patterns
- **Oxygen Saturation**: The percentage of hemoglobin binding sites occupied by oxygen

Laboratory Results: Decoding the Body's Biochemistry

This section stores the results of various diagnostic tests performed on blood, urine, or other biological specimens:

- **Blood Panels**: Comprehensive analyses revealing diverse health information from cellular components to biochemical markers
- **Urinalysis**: Assessments of kidney function and detection of potential infections or metabolic issues
- **Microbiology Tests**: Identifications of bacteria, viruses, fungi, or other microorganisms causing infection
- **Pathology Reports**: Detailed findings from tissue biopsies and other pathological examinations

Imaging Reports: Visualizing Internal Structures and Function

This category archives reports and visual data captured during various diagnostic imaging procedures:

- **X-rays**: Two-dimensional projections of bones and certain internal structures
- **CT Scans**: Detailed cross-sectional images constructed from multiple X-ray measurements
- **MRIs**: High-resolution images using magnetic fields to visualize organs, soft tissues, and bone structures
- **Ultrasound Studies**: Real-time images using sound wave technology to visualize internal organs and tissues

Progress Notes: The Clinical Narrative

This section serves as an ongoing chronological commentary on a patient's health journey, documented by various healthcare providers:

- **Symptoms**: Detailed descriptions of patient-reported symptoms and their progression
- **Physical Examination Findings**: Objective observations recorded during clinical assessments
- **Assessment and Diagnosis**: The provider's clinical interpretation and diagnostic conclusions
- **Treatment Plan**: The recommended therapeutic strategy and interventions
- **Medication Adjustments**: Any modifications made to the patient's medication regimen

Social Determinants of Health (SDOH)

This increasingly recognized category captures environmental and socioeconomic factors significantly impacting health outcomes:

- **Housing**: Quality, stability, and safety of living arrangements
- **Education**: Level of educational attainment influencing health literacy and preventive care utilization
- **Socioeconomic Status**: Income level affecting access to nutrition, healthcare, and overall wellness

- **Social Support Network**: Presence and strength of interpersonal connections contributing to physical and mental well-being

By capturing this multidimensional array of data, EHRs empower healthcare professionals in numerous ways:

- **Improved Diagnosis and Treatment Planning**: Comprehensive medical histories enable more accurate diagnoses and personalized treatment approaches. Medication lists and allergy information help prevent adverse drug events and dangerous interactions.
- **Enhanced Care Coordination**: EHRs allow healthcare providers across different settings to access complete medical records, fostering a more integrated approach to patient care.
- **Reduced Medical Error Risk**: EHR systems minimize errors through immediate access to patient histories and automated alerts for medication interactions and dosage concerns.
- **Streamlined Clinical Workflow**: EHRs automate routine documentation tasks like charting, order entry, and billing, allowing providers to dedicate more time to direct patient interaction.

This wealth of data also provides substantial value for public health initiatives and clinical research:

- **Public Health Surveillance**: Aggregated EHR data enables identification of disease trends and potential outbreaks, facilitating coordinated public health responses.
- **Healthcare Research**: Anonymized EHR data offers researchers invaluable resources for identifying disease risk factors, developing novel treatments, and evaluating existing therapeutic approaches.

However, managing such vast data repositories introduces important challenges:

- **Data Security and Privacy**: Ensuring robust protection of patient confidentiality is essential for maintaining trust in EHR systems.
- **Data Interoperability**: Different EHR platforms often struggle to communicate effectively, creating obstacles to seamless information sharing across provider organizations.
- **Data Quality**: The accuracy and completeness of entered information directly impacts the EHR's clinical utility and decision support capabilities.

Understanding the comprehensive nature of data captured in EHRs establishes the foundation for exploring how pharmaceutical companies can leverage this information for targeted marketing strategies. The next chapter will examine how organizations can utilize EHR data ethically and responsibly to engage healthcare providers with relevant information about therapeutic options.

2.2 Interoperability and Data Exchange Between Different EHR Systems

Let's revisit our earlier scenario of a patient presenting with chest pain. With a fully functional interoperability system in place:

1. The cardiologist can seamlessly access the patient's complete EHR, regardless of which system the primary care physician users
2. The specialist can immediately review the patient's medical history, including diagnoses of hypertension and hypercholesterolemia, along with their current medication regimen
3. This comprehensive information enables the cardiologist to make more informed diagnostic assessments and develop treatment strategies precisely tailored to the patient's specific health profile

Advancing interoperability will create a more connected healthcare ecosystem where patient information flows securely and seamlessly between authorized providers, ultimately elevating the quality of patient care.

Connecting the Dots in Healthcare

Imagine a patient visiting a cardiologist after experiencing concerning chest pain. To provide optimal care, the specialist needs immediate access to the patient's comprehensive medical history, including past diagnoses, medication lists, allergies, and previous test results. However, this crucial information might remain inaccessible if the patient's primary care physician utilizes an EHR system different from the one in the cardiologist's practice. This common scenario illustrates the critical importance of interoperability.

Interoperability Defined

In the healthcare context, interoperability refers to the capacity of different EHR systems to communicate and exchange patient data seamlessly across organizational boundaries. This capability ensures that authorized healthcare providers can access a patient's complete medical record regardless of which specific EHR platform they use in their practice setting.

The Importance of Data Exchange

Seamless data exchange between EHR systems delivers numerous benefits for both patients and healthcare providers:

- **Improved Continuity of Care**: With complete medical histories readily accessible, providers can make more informed decisions about diagnosis and treatment strategies
- **Reduced Medical Errors**: Access to comprehensive medication histories minimizes risks of duplicate prescriptions or potentially dangerous drug interactions
- **Enhanced Care Coordination**: Specialists and other providers involved in a patient's care can collaborate more effectively with access to shared medical records
- **Decreased Healthcare Costs**: Eliminating redundant testing and streamlining administrative processes generates significant cost savings throughout the healthcare system

Challenges of Interoperability

Despite the evident benefits, achieving true interoperability remains a significant challenge in healthcare:

- **Lack of Standardization**: Different EHR vendors employ proprietary data formats and communication protocols that hinder smooth information exchange

- **Data Security Concerns**: Sharing sensitive patient information across different systems raises legitimate concerns about maintaining data security and privacy
- **Implementation Costs**: Integrating comprehensive interoperability solutions requires substantial financial investment from healthcare institutions

Examples of Interoperability Solutions

Significant efforts are underway to overcome these challenges and promote effective interoperability:

- **HL7 Standards**: Health Level Seven (HL7) is a non-profit organization that develops widely-adopted standards for healthcare data exchange. These frameworks provide a common technical language enabling different EHR systems to communicate effectively.
- **Health Information Exchanges (HIEs)**: HIEs establish secure networks allowing authorized healthcare providers to share patient data electronically across different institutions and practice settings.
- **Fast Healthcare Interoperability Resources (FHIR)**: FHIR represents an innovative standardized data format specifically designed to enhance interoperability between diverse healthcare information systems.
- **C-CDA Standards**: Consolidated Clinical Document Architecture (C-CDA) stands as the most widely implemented format for health information exchange in the United States today. Each patient encounter can be represented by a standardized document following Clinical Document Architecture guidelines. C-CDA established stricter structural rules, encoding practices, and semantic standards to make clinical documents more readily exchangeable across systems.

Final Thoughts: The Future of EHR Functionality

The next wave of EHR advancements will integrate:

- AI-powered diagnostic tools that proactively identify potential health risks before they manifest clinically

- Seamless wearable technology synchronization enabling real-time health monitoring and data integration
- Blockchain-based security frameworks ensuring unprecedented transparency and patient control over personal health data

Organizations that strategically invest in scalable, intelligent EHR solutions will be optimally positioned to lead the future of patient-centered healthcare delivery.

What's Next

In the following chapter, we will explore critical considerations surrounding privacy and security in EHR systems, including illuminating case studies of significant data breaches and evidence-based best practices for safeguarding sensitive patient information.

Chapter Three

Ensuring Privacy and Security in EHRs

Introduction: The Critical Need for EHR Security

Imagine waking up to a notification that your entire medical history has been leaked online. Your personal diagnoses, medications, lab results, and insurance details are now accessible to cybercriminals. How would this impact your trust in digital healthcare? Would you hesitate before sharing sensitive information with your doctor in the future?

Electronic Health Records (EHRs) store some of the most sensitive data imaginable—a patient's complete medical history, treatment plans, and even genetic information. With the dramatic rise in sophisticated cyberattacks targeting healthcare institutions, implementing robust privacy and security measures is no longer optional—it's an absolute necessity.

This chapter explores:

- The evolving cybersecurity risks facing EHR systems
- How emerging technologies like AI and blockchain can enhance security
- A detailed case study on the landmark Anthem data breach and lessons learned
- A comparative analysis of traditional versus AI-powered security models
- The role of blockchain in protecting patient data integrity

As discussed in previous chapters, the widespread adoption of EHRs has revolutionized healthcare delivery. However, this digital repository of patient data also presents significant challenges regarding privacy and security that require thoughtful navigation.

The Value of Patient Data

As we explored in Chapter 2, EHRs house a wealth of sensitive information about patients, including:

- Demographics
- Medical history
- Diagnoses
- Medications
- Allergies
- Laboratory results
- Imaging reports
- Social Determinants of Health (SDOH)

This comprehensive data holds immense value for various stakeholders:

- **Healthcare Providers**: EHR data empowers clinicians to deliver more informed and coordinated care.
- **Pharmaceutical Companies**: Aggregated and anonymized EHR data can inform targeted marketing strategies for medications (a topic we'll explore in Chapter 4).
- **Public Health Agencies**: EHR data enables tracking of disease outbreaks and informs public health initiatives.
- **Researchers**: Anonymized EHR data fuels groundbreaking research to develop new treatments and improve healthcare outcomes.

Privacy Concerns

The potential benefits of EHR data are counterbalanced by legitimate privacy concerns:

- **Patient Autonomy**: Patients have the fundamental right to control their personal health information. Unrestricted access to EHR data raises concerns about potential misuse or unauthorized disclosure.
- **Stigma and Discrimination**: Certain medical conditions can lead to social stigma or discrimination. Patients may fear their health information being used against them by employers, insurers, or others.

- **Data Breaches**: Cyberattacks or accidental data breaches can compromise the security of EHR systems, exposing sensitive patient information to unauthorized parties.

Security Threats

EHR systems are particularly attractive targets for cybercriminals due to the valuable data they contain. Major security threats include:

- **Hacking**: Sophisticated cybercriminals attempt to breach EHR systems to steal patient data, which can be sold on dark web marketplaces or used for identity theft.
- **Ransomware**: Malicious software can infiltrate EHR systems, encrypting critical data and demanding ransom payments for decryption keys.
- **Insider Threats**: Authorized users within healthcare systems may misuse their legitimate access to patient data for personal gain or other improper purposes.

Navigating the Tightrope: Balancing Privacy and Security

Ensuring both robust security and patient privacy requires a multi-faceted approach:

- **Regulatory Compliance**: Government regulations such as HIPAA establish comprehensive guidelines for protecting patient privacy and data security.
- **Data Encryption**: Implementing strong encryption for patient data both at rest and in transit renders it unreadable even if intercepted by unauthorized individuals.
- **Access Controls**: Limiting access to EHR data based on the principle of least privilege ensures that only authorized personnel can access patient information relevant to their specific role.
- **Professional Education**: Thoroughly training healthcare professionals on proper data security practices and patient privacy protocols is essential.
- **Patient Empowerment**: Educating patients about their rights regarding their health information enables them to make informed decisions about data sharing.

The Road Ahead

The evolution of EHR systems presents an ongoing challenge in balancing the benefits of data utilization with the paramount need for patient privacy and security. As technology advances, so must our efforts to safeguard sensitive health information. By prioritizing robust security measures, adhering to privacy regulations, and fostering a culture of data responsibility, we can ensure that EHRs continue to serve as a powerful tool for improving healthcare delivery without compromising patient trust.

3.1 Regulatory Frameworks for Protecting Data Privacy Safeguarding Information in the Digital Age

The widespread adoption of EHRs has necessitated robust legal frameworks to protect the privacy of patients' sensitive health information. Let's examine the key regulatory initiatives governing data privacy in the context of EHRs:

Health Insurance Portability and Accountability Act (HIPAA)

HIPAA, enacted in 1996, represents the cornerstone of healthcare data privacy regulation in the United States. It establishes national standards that healthcare providers, health plans, and healthcare clearinghouses must follow when handling patients' protected health information (PHI). Key provisions include:

- **Privacy Rule**: This foundational component establishes safeguards to ensure the confidentiality of patients' PHI. It outlines specific requirements for obtaining patient authorization before using or disclosing PHI and grants patients important rights regarding their health information, including the right to access, amend, and request an accounting of disclosures.
- **Security Rule**: This critical element specifically protects the confidentiality, integrity, and availability of electronic PHI (ePHI). It mandates that healthcare entities implement appropriate administrative, physical, and technical safeguards to secure ePHI against unauthorized access or breaches.

Health Information Technology for Economic and Clinical Health Act (HITECH Act)

Enacted in 2009 as part of the American Recovery and Reinvestment Act, the HITECH Act significantly strengthened HIPAA regulations by focusing specifically on the security of electronic protected health information. Key provisions include:

- **Breach Notification Rule**: This rule requires healthcare entities to notify affected individuals and the Department of Health and Human Services (HHS) in the event of security breaches involving ePHI.
- **Enhanced Enforcement Mechanisms**: The HITECH Act substantially strengthened HIPAA's enforcement capabilities by authorizing more significant civil penalties for violations and expanding enforcement authority.

Gramm-Leach-Bliley Act (GLBA)

While not exclusively focused on healthcare, the GLBA applies to financial institutions that handle patients' health insurance information. It requires these institutions to protect the privacy and security of this data and to provide patients with access to and control over their personal information.

International Regulations

The European Union's General Data Protection Regulation (GDPR) and other international frameworks also provide significant protections for patient data privacy, particularly when handling information for patients outside the US or when data crosses international borders.

The Role of Regulatory Bodies

The Department of Health and Human Services (HHS) plays a crucial role in enforcing HIPAA regulations. HHS provides guidance and resources to help healthcare entities achieve compliance and investigates potential HIPAA violations when they occur.

The Importance of Compliance

Compliance with these regulatory frameworks represents both a legal obligation and an ethical imperative. By carefully safeguarding patient data privacy, healthcare organizations maintain patient trust and ensure the continued success of EHR systems in improving healthcare delivery.

The Road Ahead

The regulatory landscape surrounding patient data privacy continues to evolve rapidly. As technology advances and new challenges emerge, additional regulations and amendments will likely be necessary to ensure robust patient privacy protections in the digital age.

Understanding these regulatory frameworks, healthcare organizations and their partners are better equipped to navigate the ethical considerations of using EHR data for various purposes. We will explore some strategies in Chapter 4

3.2 Addressing Security Risks and Ensuring Data Integrity Building a Fortress for Patient Information

As established in previous chapters, Electronic Health Records contain extraordinary volumes of sensitive patient data. This valuable information faces vulnerability to security breaches and errors that can significantly impact patient privacy, trust in healthcare systems, and ultimately patient safety. This section explores comprehensive strategies for addressing security risks and ensuring data integrity in EHR systems.

Addressing Security Risks: Building a Multi-Layered Defense

Conceptualize an EHR system as a castle protecting sensitive patient data. Here are essential security measures that function as different layers of this defensive architecture:

- **Strong Perimeter Security**: Like castle walls, firewalls and intrusion detection/prevention systems serve as the first line of defense, filtering incoming and outgoing network traffic to block unauthorized access attempts.
- **Robust Access Controls**: Acting as gatekeepers, granular access controls restrict data availability based on a user's specific role and responsibilities. Multi-factor authentication adds a crucial additional layer by requiring supplementary verification beyond usernames and passwords.
- **Comprehensive Data Encryption**: Functioning as the vault's lock, encrypting data both at rest and in transit renders it unreadable even if intercepted by unauthorized parties. This ensures that information remains protected even if attackers breach outer security layers.
- **Regular Security Audits**: Like inspecting defenses, routine penetration testing and vulnerability assessments identify weaknesses in security posture, enabling timely remediation before exploitation.
- **Thorough User Education**: Similar to training guards, educating healthcare professionals on proper data security practices—including password hygiene and recognizing phishing attempts—is essential for maintaining strong defenses.

Examples of Security Breaches and Their Impact

- **Hacking**: In 2021, a sophisticated cyberattack on a major healthcare provider compromised the data of millions of patients. This breach resulted in stolen medical records and financial information, potentially enabling identity theft and disrupting continuity of care.

- **Insider Threats**: In 2019, a healthcare worker inappropriately accessed patient data for unauthorized purposes. This violation of patient privacy eroded trust in the healthcare system and damaged the organization's reputation.

Ensuring Data Integrity: Maintaining Accuracy and Trust

Data integrity refers to the accuracy, consistency, and reliability of information within an EHR system. Compromised data integrity can lead to misdiagnosis, inappropriate treatment plans, and ultimately patient harm. Here are key strategies to ensure data integrity:

- **Data Entry Validation**: Functioning like double-checking scrolls, implementing validation rules within EHR systems prevents errors during data entry, such as ensuring medication dosages fall within acceptable ranges.
- **Comprehensive Audit Trails**: Maintaining detailed audit logs tracks all changes made to patient data, allowing for identification and correction of errors or unauthorized modifications.
- **Regular Data Backups**: Like preserving vital records, scheduled backups of EHR data ensure its availability in case of system failures or cyberattacks. This enables continuity of care and allows for data recovery when necessary.

Examples of Data Integrity Issues and Their Impact

- **Medication Errors**: Incomplete or inaccurate medication lists in an EHR can lead to prescribing contraindicated medications or incorrect dosages, potentially causing adverse reactions.
- **Duplicate Records**: Multiple patient records containing conflicting information can create confusion and delays in care delivery.

By proactively addressing security risks and ensuring data integrity, healthcare institutions build trust with patients and ensure EHRs remain valuable tools for improving healthcare delivery. The constant vigilance required resembles maintaining a well-fortified castle, safeguarding the sensitive information entrusted to the healthcare system.

With robust security measures and unwavering commitment to data integrity, we can unlock the full potential of EHRs, enabling advancements in personalized medicine, research, and ultimately better health outcomes.

3.3 Building Trust and Transparency in the Use of EHR Data Balancing Progress with Patient Privacy

Electronic Health Records contain extraordinarily valuable data for improving healthcare outcomes. However, leveraging this information effectively requires building sustained trust and transparency with patients. This section explores strategies to achieve this delicate balance.

Transparency: Shining Light on Data Practices

Transparency involves being open and honest with patients about how their EHR data is used. Healthcare institutions can achieve this through:

- **Clear and Accessible Privacy Policies**: Patients have the fundamental right to understand how their data is collected, used, and shared. Easy-to-comprehend privacy policies outlining these practices in plain language are essential.
- **Comprehensive Patient Education**: Informing patients about the potential benefits of EHR data use—such as improved care coordination and research advancements—fosters trust and understanding about why data sharing matters.
- **Meaningful Opt-Out Options**: Patients should have the clearly communicated right to opt out of having their data used for certain purposes, such as targeted marketing by pharmaceutical companies.

Example: A forward-thinking hospital implements a patient portal feature that allows individuals to easily access detailed explanations of how their EHR data is used for research purposes. This transparency empowers patients to make informed decisions about data sharing.

Building Trust: Earning Patient Confidence

Building trust extends beyond merely informing patients. Here are essential steps healthcare institutions can take:

- **Demonstrating Privacy Commitment**: Building trust requires visible commitment to data security and privacy through robust security measures and strict adherence to regulatory frameworks.
- **Responsive Concern Management**: Actively listening to and addressing patient concerns regarding data privacy demonstrates respect for their autonomy and builds confidence in the system.
- **Meaningful Patient Involvement**: Including patient representatives in discussions about data use policies fosters a sense of partnership and empowers patients to influence how their information is utilized.

Example: A community clinic hosts regular open forums to discuss how EHR data supports local public health initiatives. Patients can ask questions and learn about the safeguards protecting their privacy. This two-way communication builds trust through direct engagement.

The Role of Regulation

As discussed in section 3.1, government regulations like HIPAA establish crucial baseline standards for protecting patient privacy. However, building genuine trust requires healthcare organizations to go beyond merely meeting minimum compliance requirements.

The Power of Collaboration

Building trust and transparency requires coordinated effort among various stakeholders:

- **Healthcare Institutions**: Implementing strong data governance practices and prioritizing patient privacy in organizational culture.
- **Technology Vendors**: Developing secure, user-friendly EHR systems that empower patients to understand and manage their data permissions.
- **Policymakers**: Enacting regulations that balance innovation with robust patient privacy protections.

The Road Ahead

The landscape of EHR data utilization continues to evolve rapidly. By prioritizing transparency, building trust, and fostering collaboration, healthcare organizations can ensure that EHR data serves as a powerful tool for improving care delivery while safeguarding patient privacy.

Examples of Consequences of Breached Trust

- **Erosion of Patient Confidence**: News of a significant data breach at a healthcare institution can undermine patient trust in the entire system, potentially leading to delayed or avoided necessary care.
- **Reduced Data Sharing Willingness**: Patients who distrust how their data is used become less willing to share information, hindering research efforts and innovation.

Building trust and transparency in the use of EHR data represents both an ethical imperative and a strategic necessity. By prioritizing patient privacy and fostering open communication, healthcare institutions can unlock the full potential of EHR data while maintaining the trust of the patients they serve.

The Growing Threat to Healthcare Data Security

The healthcare industry has emerged as the primary target for cybercriminals, surpassing even financial institutions in attack frequency. A single sophisticated data breach can expose millions of patient records, potentially leading to identity theft, fraudulent insurance claims, and devastating loss of patient trust.

Key Cybersecurity Threats in EHR Systems

Threat Type	Description	Impact
Ransomware Attacks	Cybercriminals encrypt hospital data and demand payment for its release	Healthcare operations disrupted, delaying critical patient care
Insider Threats	Employees misuse or sell patient data for financial gain	Patient privacy compromised, leading to legal liability and reputational damage
Data Breaches	Insufficient security measures allow hackers to steal sensitive patient information	Millions of records potentially leaked, enabling identity theft
IoT & Wearable Device Vulnerabilities	Remote patient monitoring devices introduce additional entry points for cyberattacks	Hackers can potentially manipulate health data or disable critical alerts

FIGURE 3.1: Cyber Security Threats in EHR Systems.

Key Takeaway: Without implementing robust encryption, multi-factor authentication, and AI-powered threat detection systems, healthcare organizations remain vulnerable to potentially devastating breaches with far-reaching consequences.

Case Study: The $16M Anthem Data Breach – A Hard Lesson in Cybersecurity

The Problem: Inadequate Security Controls Led to a Massive Breach

In 2015, Anthem Inc., the second-largest health insurer in the United States, suffered a catastrophic cyberattack that exposed 80 million patient records. The breach occurred due to several critical security failures:

- Compromised administrator credentials, allowing attackers to gain unauthorized system access
- Lack of comprehensive data encryption, meaning stolen information was easily readable
- Insufficient security policies and enforcement, leaving patient records unnecessarily vulnerable

The consequences were severe and far-reaching:

- $16 million in federal fines for HIPAA violations
- Significant erosion of consumer trust, leading to measurable decline in membership renewals
- Multiple class-action lawsuits, costing Anthem additional millions in settlements

How Anthem Strengthened Its EHR Security

Following this watershed breach, Anthem implemented comprehensive security improvements:

- **Multi-Factor Authentication (MFA)** – Requiring additional verification layers beyond passwords for system access
- **AI-Powered Intrusion Detection Systems** – Deploying real-time monitoring to identify and flag suspicious activity patterns
- **Comprehensive Data Encryption** – Protecting all sensitive records both in transit and at rest
- **Enhanced Employee Cybersecurity Training** – Educating staff to recognize phishing attacks and follow proper data handling protocols

Contd...

The Outcome: A More Secure Digital Healthcare Environment

- Zero major data breaches reported since implementing comprehensive security upgrades
- 99% phishing attack detection success rate using AI-driven monitoring systems
- $75 million in projected fraud prevention savings anticipated over the next decade

Key Takeaway: Robust cybersecurity in EHR systems is non-negotiable—a single significant breach can lead to massive financial penalties, reputational damage, and loss of patient trust.

Comparison: Traditional Security vs. AI-Powered Cybersecurity

Security Measure	Traditional Approach	AI-Powered Approach
Threat Detection	Reactive (manual security checks)	Proactive (continuous real-time AI monitoring)
User Authentication	Simple password-based logins	Multi-factor authentication with biometrics & AI risk assessment
Data Encryption	Standard encryption methods	Advanced encryption with AI anomaly detection
Insider Threats	Periodic manual audits of user activity	AI-driven behavioral analysis to detect suspicious employee actions
Incident Response	Human-initiated security alerts	Automated AI-driven responses to immediately block threats

FIGURE 3.2: Comparison Table – Traditional vs. AI-Powered Cybersecurity in EHRs.

How Blockchain Enhances EHR Security

In the rapidly evolving landscape of healthcare information technology, the security and privacy of Electronic Health Records remain paramount concerns. Blockchain technology offers promising solutions for enhancing protection of sensitive patient data by preventing unauthorized access while maintaining appropriate availability for legitimate uses.

By leveraging blockchain's decentralized and immutable architecture, healthcare providers can ensure patient information remains secure while still allowing controlled access by authorized personnel.

Introduction to EHRs and Their Vulnerabilities

As explored in previous chapters, Electronic Health Records represent digital versions of patients' paper charts and are essential for modern healthcare delivery. However, the centralized nature of traditional EHR systems creates inherent vulnerability to data breaches and unauthorized access. Cyberattacks, insider threats, and inadequate security measures can expose sensitive patient information, leading to severe consequences for both patients and healthcare providers.

The Role of Blockchain in Data Security

Blockchain technology offers a promising solution to challenges faced by conventional EHR systems. Using a decentralized ledger architecture, blockchain ensures that data isn't stored in a single location, making unauthorized access or manipulation significantly more difficult. Key security features include:

Decentralization

In a blockchain network, patient data is distributed across multiple nodes rather than being stored in a central database. This distributed approach eliminates single points of failure and creates substantial barriers for potential attackers attempting to compromise the entire system.

Immutability

Once information is recorded on a blockchain, it cannot be altered or deleted without consensus from network participants. This immutability ensures patient records remain intact and trustworthy, preventing unauthorized modifications that could compromise care quality.

Cryptographic Security

Blockchain employs sophisticated cryptographic techniques to secure data. Each transaction is encrypted and linked to previous entries, creating a secure information chain. This encryption protects patient data from unauthorized access and ensures only those with proper decryption keys can view sensitive information.

Smart Contracts

Smart contracts represent self-executing agreements with terms directly encoded in computer code. For EHR applications, smart contracts can automate access permissions, allowing only authorized users to access specific data based on predefined criteria. This adds an essential layer of security and granular control over patient information.

Controlled Access and Patient Consent

Blockchain technology facilitates patient-controlled access to EHRs by enabling individuals to manage their own data permissions. Patients can grant or revoke access rights to their health records through secure blockchain interfaces, ensuring only authorized healthcare providers can view their information. This patient-centric approach enhances privacy while empowering individuals to control their health data.

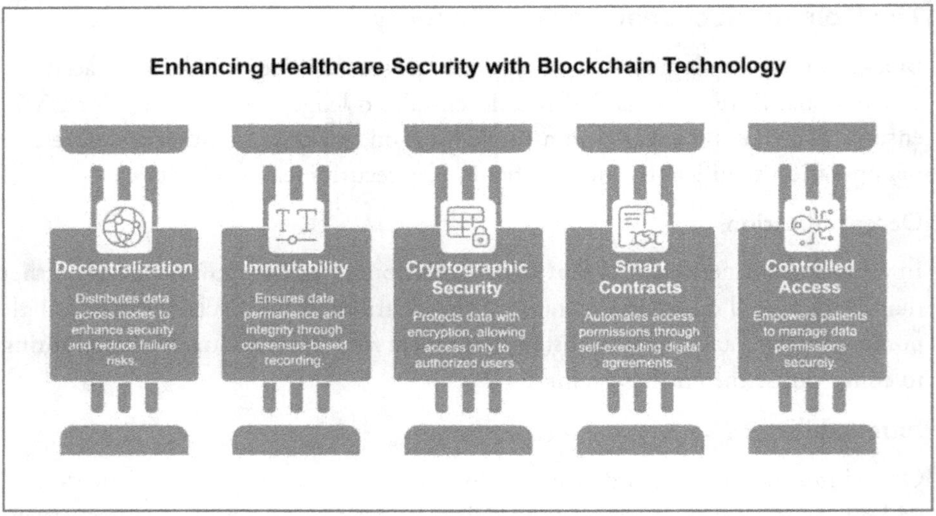

FIGURE 3.3: Enhancing Healthcare Security with Blockchain Technology.

Best Practices: Strengthening EHR Security

Healthcare organizations can implement these evidence-based practices to enhance EHR security:

- **Implement Zero-Trust Security Frameworks** – Assume that every user and device represents a potential threat until verified through multiple factors.
- **Deploy AI-Based Anomaly Detection** – Utilize AI-driven systems to monitor login patterns and flag suspicious activity that deviates from established baselines.

- **Encrypt All Patient Data** – Ensure comprehensive encryption protection for data both at rest and in transit through the network.
- **Adopt Blockchain for Data Integrity** – Implement decentralized ledger systems to ensure tamper-proof health records.
- **Strengthen Multi-Factor Authentication (MFA)** – Require multiple authentication factors for secure system access.

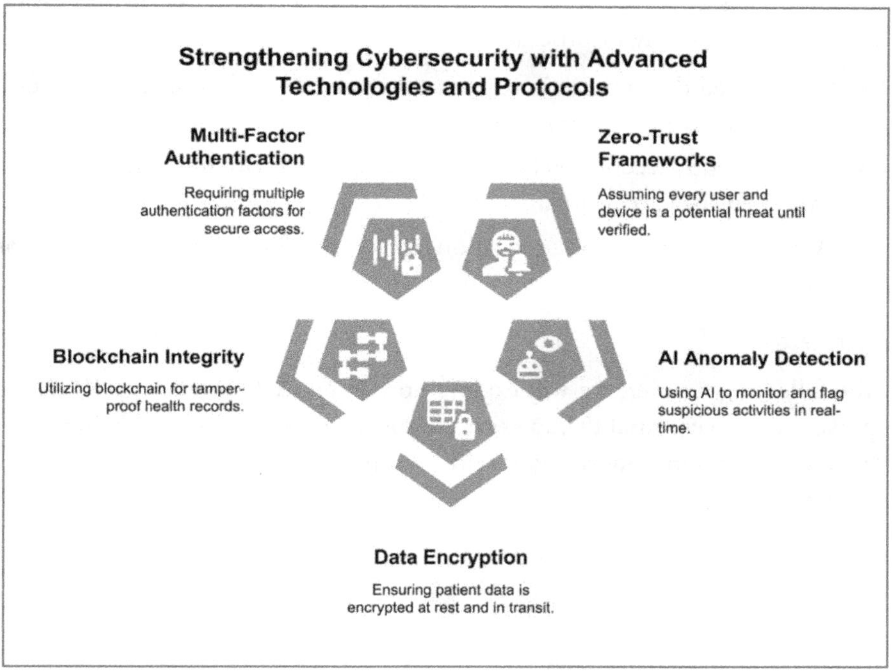

FIGURE 3.4: Strengthening Cybersecurity with Advanced Technologies and Protocols.

- **Conduct Regular Cybersecurity Audits** – Systematically assess vulnerabilities and update security policies to address emerging threats.
- **Educate Employees on Security Best Practices** – Provide comprehensive training to reduce phishing susceptibility and mitigate insider threats.
- **Implement Secure Cloud Backups** – Store patient data with robust encryption to prevent ransomware attacks from causing permanent data loss.

- **Monitor and Restrict Third-Party Access** – Thoroughly vet all external vendors for compliance with security policies before granting system access.
- **Develop Comprehensive Incident Response Plans** – Establish detailed protocols for immediate action in case of security breaches.

Final Thoughts: The Future of EHR Security

As cyber threats continue to evolve in sophistication, the next phase of EHR security will increasingly incorporate:

- AI-powered threat detection systems that predict and mitigate cyberattacks before data compromise occurs
- Fully decentralized blockchain networks that give patients complete control over their data access permissions
- Advanced biometric authentication replacing traditional passwords for more secure system access

Whats Next

In the following chapter, we will explore how to ethically leverage EHR data to improve access to essential therapies and support responsible awareness initiatives, balancing innovation opportunities with an unwavering commitment to patient privacy protection.

Chapter Four

Unveiling Patient Insights for Targeted Marketing

The Power and Responsibility of EHR Data

For pharmaceutical companies, Electronic Health Records (EHRs) offer unprecedented opportunities to analyze real-world patient data, enhance drug development processes, and craft more effective marketing strategies. However, this powerful capability comes with significant responsibility: How can organizations ethically use patient insights while ensuring strict compliance with privacy regulations?

A Marketer's Dilemma:
The Balance Between Innovation and Privacy

Meet Lisa Carter, a pharmaceutical marketing executive at a global healthcare company. Her team recently launched an innovative diabetes medication, and she's tasked with increasing physician awareness and patient adoption.

Lisa's company has access to de-identified EHR data revealing the geographic distribution of diabetes patients, their treatment histories, and apparent gaps in care delivery. This information could inform targeted educational materials for healthcare providers who treat these patient populations.

However, Lisa faces important ethical and legal challenges:

- How can she leverage EHR insights without violating patient privacy laws?
- Can AI-powered marketing enhance patient care, or might it become overly intrusive?
- Where should the line be drawn between patient-centered education and data-driven advertising?

Lisa's dilemma reflects a larger industry challenge: How can pharmaceutical companies harness real-world evidence (RWE) responsibly while maintaining public trust and regulatory compliance?

Case Study: Pfizer's Use of Real-World Evidence (RWE) for Drug Expansion

The Problem: A Need for Real-World Data

Pfizer sought to expand indications for its rheumatoid arthritis drug, Xeljanz, but lacked sufficient long-term cardiovascular risk data from traditional clinical trials. Regulatory approval required evidence beyond controlled studies, demonstrating how the drug performed across diverse patient populations in real-world settings.

As we explored in Chapters 1 and 2, Electronic Health Records have revolutionized healthcare delivery by offering comprehensive views of patients' medical histories. This rich data landscape holds immense value for the pharmaceutical industry, enabling more targeted marketing strategies. However, navigating privacy concerns and adhering to ethical principles remains essential for responsible utilization.

Unveiling the Power of Patient Insights

EHR data provides a unique window into patient demographics, diagnoses, medications, laboratory results, and treatment trajectories. By analyzing this information responsibly, pharmaceutical companies can gain valuable insights into:

- **Patient Needs**: Identifying specific population segments with conditions that new medications could effectively address.
- **Treatment Patterns**: Understanding current prescribing trends for similar medications within particular specialties.
- **Medication Gaps**: Detecting patients who might benefit from specific treatments but haven't received appropriate prescriptions.
- **Real-World Effectiveness**: Analyzing how existing medications perform in actual clinical settings beyond controlled trials.

Targeted Marketing Strategies in Action

Here's how pharmaceutical companies can leverage EHR data to develop focused marketing campaigns that reach the right healthcare providers with relevant information:

- **Disease Awareness Campaigns**: A company developing a new diabetes medication can identify primary care physicians with large diabetic patient populations and target them with educational materials about the medication's benefits and potential role in comprehensive treatment plans.

Contd...

- **Comparative Effectiveness Messaging**: For a new cholesterol medication, EHR data can identify cardiologists who frequently prescribe competitors' products. Marketing efforts can then highlight the new medication's unique advantages based on clinical trial results.
- **Reimbursement and Adherence Support**: Marketing materials can address specific HCP concerns by providing information on insurance coverage pathways or offering patient adherence support programs.

Example: A pharmaceutical company develops a breakthrough treatment for a rare cancer subtype. By analyzing EHR data, they identify oncologists who have treated patients with this specific diagnosis. The company then delivers educational materials to these specialists about the new medication's efficacy profile, potentially enabling earlier intervention for patients with this rare condition.

Ethical Considerations and Privacy Concerns

While EHR data offers significant benefits, prioritizing patient privacy and ethical considerations remains paramount:

- **Patient Consent**: Individuals should have the right to opt out of having their data used for marketing purposes.
- **Data Anonymization**: EHR information used for marketing campaigns must be thoroughly de-identified to protect patient privacy.
- **Transparency**: Pharmaceutical companies should maintain transparency about how they collect, analyze, and utilize EHR data.
- **Physician Autonomy**: Marketing efforts should inform healthcare providers rather than attempt to dictate prescribing decisions. Medication selection ultimately remains with physicians based on their professional judgment and individual patient needs.

How Pfizer Leveraged EHR Data

Pfizer partnered with leading health data companies Cerner and Optum, accessing de-identified EHR data from more than 500,000 patients to:

- Analyze medication adherence patterns in real-world settings
- Assess cardiovascular side effects across diverse patient demographics
- Compare effectiveness against other arthritis treatments to evaluate safety profiles

The Outcome: Evidence-Driven Drug Expansion

- New FDA-approved indication for cardiovascular risk reduction
- $750 million in additional revenue from expanded therapeutic applications
- Lower off-label prescribing rates, improving treatment accuracy and patient safety

Key Takeaway: EHR-driven real-world evidence studies can accelerate regulatory approvals and ensure safer, more effective therapeutic applications.

How EHR Data Powers Ethical Pharma Marketing

In the rapidly evolving pharmaceutical marketing landscape, Electronic Health Record data integration has become a transformative force. This section explores the ethical implications and advantages of utilizing EHR data in pharmaceutical marketing strategies. By responsibly leveraging comprehensive patient information, pharmaceutical companies can enhance their marketing approaches while ensuring compliance with ethical standards and improving patient outcomes.

Understanding EHR Data

As detailed in Chapter 2, Electronic Health Records contain a wealth of clinical information, including medical history, diagnoses, medications, treatment plans, immunization records, allergies, imaging studies, and laboratory results.

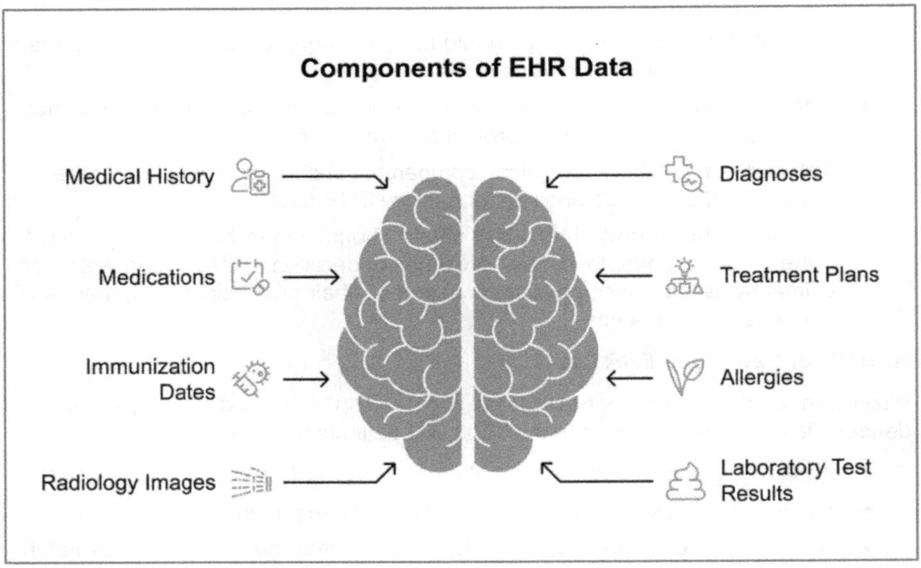

FIGURE 4.1: Components of EHR Data.

This comprehensive data provides invaluable insights for pharmaceutical companies seeking to understand patient needs and tailor marketing strategies accordingly.

Ethical Considerations in Pharma Marketing

Ethical pharmaceutical marketing is essential for maintaining trust among healthcare providers, patients, and pharmaceutical companies. The use of EHR data must adhere to strict guidelines to protect patient privacy and ensure marketing practices don't compromise care quality. Key ethical considerations include:

- **Patient Privacy**: Rigorous compliance with regulations such as HIPAA is essential for safeguarding sensitive patient information.
- **Informed Consent**: Patients should receive clear information about how their data might be used and have straightforward opt-out options.
- **Transparency**: Pharmaceutical companies must maintain transparency regarding their marketing practices and data sources.

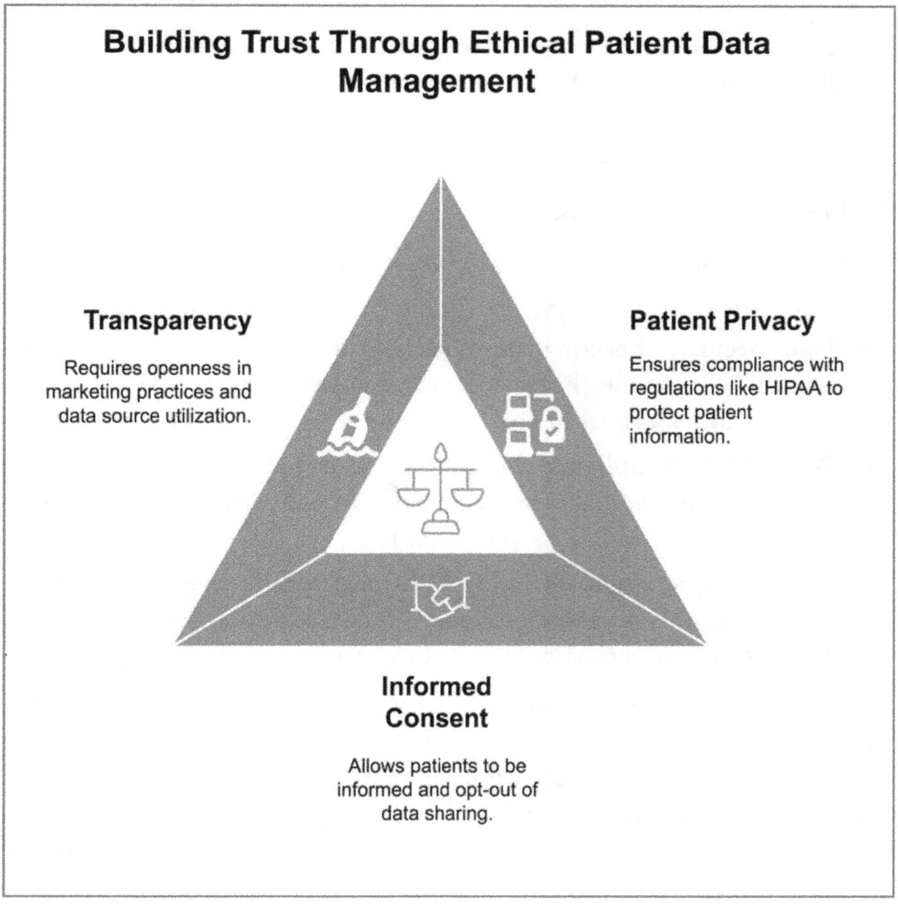

FIGURE 4.2: Building Trust through Ethical Patient Data Management.

Benefits of EHR Data in Pharma Marketing

- **Targeted Marketing**: EHR data enables pharmaceutical companies to identify specific patient populations that could benefit from their products, creating more relevant and effective marketing campaigns.
- **Improved Patient Outcomes**: By understanding patient demographics and clinical conditions, pharmaceutical companies can develop educational content that empowers patients to make informed healthcare decisions.
- **Enhanced Collaboration with Providers**: EHR data facilitates more meaningful communication between pharmaceutical representatives and healthcare providers, enabling collaborative approaches to improving patient care.
- **Real-Time Insights**: Access to current data allows pharmaceutical companies to adapt marketing strategies quickly based on emerging trends and evolving patient needs.

Challenges and Solutions

While EHR data offers significant marketing advantages, it also presents important challenges:

- **Data Security**: Ensuring the protection of sensitive patient information remains paramount. Pharmaceutical companies must invest in robust cybersecurity measures to prevent data breaches.
- **Regulatory Compliance**: Navigating the complex healthcare regulatory landscape requires diligence. Companies should partner with legal experts to ensure compliance with all relevant laws.
- **Data Interpretation**: Analyzing EHR data requires specialized expertise. Pharmaceutical organizations may need dedicated data analysts or partnerships with analytics firms to extract actionable insights.

The integration of EHR data into pharmaceutical marketing represents a significant opportunity for enhancing ethical practices and improving patient outcomes. By prioritizing privacy, ensuring transparency, and adhering to ethical guidelines, pharmaceutical companies can leverage EHR data to create more effective marketing campaigns that benefit both patients and healthcare providers.

EHRs provide critical insights into patient behavior, treatment efficacy, and disease progression. When used responsibly, this data can:

- Identify underserved patient populations that could benefit from new therapies
- Support evidence-based physician education through real-world treatment trends
- Enhance drug safety monitoring by tracking adverse reactions across patient cohorts

However, misusing EHR data can lead to serious ethical and legal consequences. To balance these factors, companies should follow this structured approach:

Step Process Ethical Considerations

1. Data Collection | Gather de-identified patient data from EHRs | Ensure compliance with HIPAA & GDPR requirements
2. Patient Segmentation | Identify trends in treatment efficacy and unmet needs | Avoid overly specific targeting that could potentially re-identify patients
3. Physician Engagement | Educate HCPs with evidence-based insights | Focus on medical education rather than promotional pressure
4. Marketing Campaigns | Create awareness about new treatment options | Use anonymized data to inform strategy development
5. Compliance Monitoring | Regularly audit data usage and adjust policies as needed | Continuously review adherence to evolving privacy laws

Step	Process	Ethical Considerations
1. Data Collection	Gather de-identified patient data from EHRs.	Ensure compliance with HIPAA & GDPR.
2. Patient Segmentation	Identify trends in treatment efficacy and unmet needs.	Avoid overly specific targeting that could re-identify patients.
3. Physician Engagement	Educate HCPs with evidence-based insights.	Focus on medical education, not promotional pressure.
4. Marketing Campaigns	Create awareness about new treatment options.	Use anonymized data to inform strategy.
5. Compliance Monitoring	Audit data usage and adjust policies as needed.	Regularly review adherence to privacy laws.

FIGURE 4.3: How EHR Powers Ethical Data Use for Marketing.

***Key Takeaway*:** Transparency, compliance, and patient benefit should guide all EHR-driven marketing initiatives.

Addressing Privacy Concerns

As discussed in Chapter 3, regulations like HIPAA establish important guidelines for protecting patient privacy. Here are strategies to ensure responsible use of EHR data for marketing:

- **Partnerships with Privacy-Focused EHR Vendors**: Collaborating with EHR vendors who prioritize robust data security and anonymization processes.
- **Focus on Aggregate Trends**: Marketing strategies should analyze patterns within large datasets rather than targeting individual patients.
- **Utilize De-identified Data Sets**: Working exclusively with properly de-identified data that eliminates linkable patient information.

The Road Ahead: A Future Focused on Value and Outcomes

The use of EHR data for pharmaceutical marketing continues to evolve. As technology advances and regulations adapt, we can anticipate these emerging trends:

- **Advanced Data Analytics**: Increasingly sophisticated analytics will enable more precise targeting and deeper insights from EHR data.
- **Comprehensive Real-World Data Integration**: Combining EHR data with other real-world information sources like claims databases will provide more complete understanding of medication effectiveness and safety.
- **Value-Based Marketing Focus**: Marketing efforts will increasingly emphasize medications' value propositions, including cost-effectiveness and improved patient outcomes.

EHR data represents a powerful resource for developing targeted marketing strategies in the pharmaceutical industry. By prioritizing patient privacy, adhering to ethical principles, and focusing on providing healthcare providers with valuable information, pharmaceutical companies can leverage EHR data responsibly to improve patient care and medication utilization.

Ethical vs Unethical Use of EHR Data in Marketing

EHR data must be used responsibly to prevent privacy violations, inappropriate targeting, and erosion of patient trust. Below is a comparison of ethical versus unethical marketing practices:

Comparison Table – Ethical vs. Unethical Use of Patient Data

Criteria	Ethical Use	Unethical Use
Data Transparency	Patients and providers receive clear information about data utilization	Data collection and usage occurs without patient knowledge
Marketing Approach	Focuses on education, disease awareness, and improving care	Directly targets individual patients based on their medical history
Privacy Protection	Uses only properly de-identified, aggregate data	Utilizes personally identifiable patient information without consent
Regulatory Compliance	Strictly adheres to HIPAA, GDPR, and all applicable regulations	Circumvents regulations to maximize sales potential
HCP Engagement	Provides physicians with evidence-based treatment insights	Pressures healthcare providers to
HCP Engagement	Provides physicians with evidence-based treatment insights	Pressures healthcare providers to prescribe specific medications regardless of patient needs
Outcome Focus	Emphasizes improving patient care and health outcomes	Prioritizes sales and market share above patient wellbeing
Data Governance	Implements strict controls on data access and usage	Allows broad access to patient data without appropriate safeguards

FIGURE 4.4: Ethical vs Unethical Use of EHR Data in Marketing.

***Key Takeaway*:** Ethical marketing prioritizes education, transparency, and patient wellbeing, while unethical practices subordinate privacy to commercial interests.

Checklist: Ensuring Compliance in EHR-Based Marketing

To maintain ethical marketing strategies, pharmaceutical companies should implement these essential best practices:

- ✓ Obtain explicit patient consent where required by applicable regulations
- ✓ Ensure all patient data is thoroughly de-identified before utilization
- ✓ Adhere strictly to HIPAA, GDPR, and local data protection laws
- ✓ Avoid direct-to-consumer marketing using EHR data—focus instead on healthcare provider education
- ✓ Conduct regular compliance audits to verify ongoing adherence to regulations
- ✓ Maintain transparency about data usage—healthcare providers and patients should understand how insights are developed

***Key Takeaway*:** Compliance represents not merely a legal requirement but an essential foundation for maintaining patient trust and long-term organizational credibility.

4.1 Leveraging Patient Demographics and Medical History for Targeted Outreach

The Right Message, Delivered to the Right Patient

In contemporary healthcare, reaching appropriate patients with relevant messages at optimal times can significantly impact preventive care, treatment adherence, and overall health outcomes. Patient demographics and medical history captured in Electronic Health Records offer valuable insights for developing precisely targeted outreach campaigns.

Unlocking the Power of Demographics and Medical History

Broad outreach strategies can utilize basic patient demographics, including age, gender, location, and socioeconomic indicators:

- **Age-Specific Campaigns**: Implementing reminders about age-appropriate screenings such as mammograms for women over 40 or colonoscopies for adults over 50.
- **Location-Based Outreach**: Targeting communities with elevated rates of specific conditions to promote educational resources or vaccination initiatives.
- **Socioeconomic Considerations**: Offering accessible health screenings in underserved communities to address healthcare disparities.

Medical history enables a more sophisticated approach based on specific patient health needs:

- **Chronic Disease Management**: Connecting with diabetic patients to provide medication adherence reminders or blood glucose monitoring support.
- **Preventive Care**: Encouraging patients with hypertension to schedule follow-up appointments for medication adjustments or lifestyle modification counseling.
- **Post-Treatment Follow-up**: Contacting patients after hospitalization to ensure proper recovery and medication adherence.

Examples of Targeted Outreach in Action

1. A regional hospital identifies a significant cluster of asthma cases within a specific zip code. They launch a targeted social media campaign in that area, promoting a free educational seminar on asthma management for local residents.
2. A healthcare system identifies patients overdue for routine preventive examinations. The provider sends personalized email reminders highlighting the importance of these screenings for early detection of potential health concerns.
3. Patients with documented heart disease receive automated appointment reminders prompting them to schedule annual cardiac evaluations based on their risk profiles.

Beyond Basic Demographics and Medical History

While demographics and medical history provide a strong foundation, incorporating additional contextual information can further enhance outreach effectiveness:

- **Lifestyle Factors**: If a patient's EHR indicates tobacco use, they might receive targeted information about smoking cessation programs aligned with their specific health profile.
- **Behavioral Patterns**: Understanding a patient's history of appointment adherence can inform communication strategy, with appropriately calibrated reminders for those who frequently miss appointments.

The Importance of Patient Preferences

When designing outreach campaigns, considering a patient's preferred communication channel (email, text, phone) significantly improves engagement. Additionally, providing straightforward opt-out mechanisms fosters trust and respects individual privacy preferences.

The Benefits of Targeted Outreach

- **Improved Patient Engagement**: Relevant, personalized messages resonate more effectively with patients, increasing participation in preventive care and treatment programs.
- **Enhanced Clinical Outcomes**: Early detection of health concerns and improved treatment adherence directly translate to better patient outcomes.
- **Optimized Healthcare Resources**: Preventive interventions generally cost less than managing advanced disease states, creating system-wide efficiencies.

Ethical Considerations and Privacy Concerns

Patient privacy and ethical considerations remain paramount in targeted outreach:

- **Regulatory Compliance**: All outreach efforts must adhere to privacy regulations discussed in Chapter 3, particularly HIPAA requirements.
- **Data Security**: Implementing robust protection measures safeguards patient information from unauthorized access.

- **Transparency**: Patients should receive clear information about how their data informs outreach programs, with straightforward opt-out options.

The Future of Targeted Outreach

Advancements in data analytics and artificial intelligence continue to enhance targeted outreach capabilities:

- **Predictive Modeling**: Identifying patients at elevated risk for specific conditions enables proactive interventions before disease progression.
- **Personalized Communication**: Tailoring message content, timing, and delivery channels to individual preferences maximizes engagement effectiveness.
- **Real-Time Intervention**: Integrating wearable devices and remote monitoring systems enables timely outreach based on real-time health indicators.

4.2 Identifying Patient Cohorts and Understanding Treatment Patterns

Unveiling Insights from EHR Data

Electronic Health Records contain extensive patient information that can identify distinct patient groups (cohorts) and reveal treatment approaches for specific conditions. This knowledge provides valuable insights for researchers, healthcare providers, and policymakers seeking to improve care delivery and patient outcomes.

Identifying Patient Cohorts

Conceptualize EHR data as an extensive library of patient medical histories. Researchers leverage this information to identify distinct patient cohorts through:

- **Diagnostic Codes**: Using International Classification of Diseases (ICD) codes to identify patients with specific conditions, from diabetes to heart failure to particular cancer types.
- **Laboratory Values**: Analyzing specific test results to define cohorts based on biomarker presence or absence.

- **Demographic Factors**: Grouping patients by age, gender, ethnicity, or socioeconomic indicators to identify disparities in treatment patterns or disease prevalence.
- **Treatment History**: Identifying patients who received particular medications or procedures to study effectiveness and potential side effects within defined populations.

Examples of Patient Cohort Identification

- Researchers studying long-term effects of a novel diabetes treatment might identify a cohort of patients diagnosed with Type 2 diabetes within the past 12 months.
- Public health officials could analyze EHR data to identify pregnant women who haven't received recommended vaccinations, creating a targeted outreach cohort.
- Healthcare systems might examine treatment patterns for heart failure patients over 65, comparing medication utilization and outcomes with younger populations.

Understanding Treatment Patterns

Once cohorts are identified, EHR data enables deeper analysis of treatment approaches:

- **Medication Utilization**: Examining medication types, dosages, and combinations prescribed within a cohort reveals common treatment approaches and potential prescribing variations.
- **Hospitalization Frequency**: Comparing hospitalization rates within cohorts can indicate treatment plan effectiveness in managing specific conditions.
- **Treatment Adherence**: Tracking medication refills and regimen compliance helps assess real-world treatment effectiveness beyond controlled clinical settings.
- **Clinical Outcomes**: Analyzing disease progression, treatment response, and mortality rates within cohorts provides insights into different treatment approaches' efficacy.

Examples of Treatment Pattern Analysis

- Researchers might examine a depression patient cohort and identify significant regional variations in antidepressant prescribing patterns.
- Healthcare systems could analyze asthma patient cohorts to identify subgroups with higher hospitalization rates, prompting investigation into contributing factors.
- Oncology researchers might discover specific treatment combinations that improve survival rates by studying cancer patient cohorts.

Benefits of Cohort Identification and Treatment Pattern Analysis

- **Enhanced Clinical Research**: Well-defined patient cohorts enable more focused and statistically robust clinical trials.
- **Personalized Medicine Advancement**: Understanding treatment variations supports developing individualized treatment approaches based on patient characteristics.
- **Comparative Effectiveness Research**: Comparing outcomes across different cohorts helps identify optimal approaches for specific patient populations.
- **Resource Optimization**: Analyzing treatment patterns reveals opportunities for efficiency improvements and cost-effective interventions.

Challenges and Considerations

- **Data Quality**: The accuracy and completeness of EHR data directly impact analysis reliability.
- **Privacy Protection**: Patient confidentiality must be safeguarded in all research utilizing EHR data.
- **Generalizability Limitations**: Findings from specific cohorts may not apply universally across broader populations.

The Future of Cohort Analysis and Treatment Pattern Research

EHR-based cohort identification and treatment pattern analysis continue evolving rapidly:

- **Integrated Real-World Data**: Combining EHR information with claims databases and patient-reported outcomes provides more comprehensive effectiveness insights.
- **Advanced AI Applications**: Artificial intelligence algorithms analyzing vast EHR datasets can identify previously unrecognized patterns and relationships within patient cohorts.
- **Precision Medicine Implementation**: Sophisticated analytics increasingly enable treatment personalization based on genetic profiles and other individual factors.

4.3 Utilizing Real-World Data (RWD) from EHRs for Drug Development and Marketing

Electronic Health Records represent an invaluable source of real-world data (RWD) with applications across the pharmaceutical value chain. This information provides insights beyond controlled clinical trial environments, enhancing drug development and marketing strategies while necessitating careful attention to ethical considerations.

The Power of RWD in Drug Development

Real-world data from EHRs complements traditional clinical trials by providing broader perspectives on drug effectiveness and safety in diverse populations:

- **Novel Target Identification**: Analyzing EHR data patterns of disease progression and treatment response can reveal potential new drug targets.
- **Optimized Clinical Trial Patient Selection**: EHR data helps identify patients meeting specific criteria for clinical trials, creating more representative study populations.
- **Enhanced Safety Monitoring**: Analyzing large patient datasets using specific medications in real-world settings helps detect rare adverse events that might not appear in smaller clinical trials.
- **Comprehensive Post-Marketing Surveillance**: After market introduction, EHR data enables ongoing monitoring of long-term safety and effectiveness.

Example: A pharmaceutical company developing a diabetes treatment might utilize EHR data to identify patients with specific genetic or biomarker profiles likely to respond optimally to the medication. This information can inform patient selection for Phase II clinical trials, potentially improving success rates.

RWD in Pharmaceutical Marketing: Delivering Relevant Information

EHR data can inform targeted marketing strategies that provide valuable information to appropriate healthcare providers:

- **Identifying Relevant Patient Populations**: Analyzing demographics and diagnostic patterns within EHR data helps identify patient groups potentially benefiting from specific medications.
- **Understanding Prescribing Patterns**: RWD reveals how similar medications are currently prescribed, enabling focused messaging about a new drug's unique advantages.
- **Developing Evidence-Based Educational Materials**: EHR data insights inform educational content highlighting real-world benefits of medications on patient outcomes.

Example: A company launching a new cholesterol medication might analyze EHR data to identify cardiologists frequently prescribing similar therapies. Marketing efforts can then focus on providing these specialists with evidence-based materials demonstrating the new medication's potential advantages for specific patient populations.

Ethical Considerations and Privacy Protections

Utilizing real-world data for drug development and marketing requires careful attention to ethical principles and patient privacy:

- **Informed Consent**: Patients should understand how their data might be used and have appropriate opt-out options.
- **Thorough De-identification**: RWD used for marketing or research must be properly anonymized to protect patient confidentiality.
- **Transparent Practices**: Pharmaceutical companies should maintain openness about how they collect, analyze, and utilize real-world data.

- **Provider Education Focus**: Marketing efforts should aim to educate healthcare providers rather than influence prescribing decisions inappropriately.

Addressing Privacy Concerns

Building on privacy principles discussed in Chapter 3, regulations like HIPAA provide essential guidelines for protecting patient privacy. Responsible use of EHR data includes:

- **Partnerships with Privacy-Focused Vendors**: Collaborating with EHR providers prioritizing robust security and de-identification protocols.
- **Population-Level Analysis**: Focusing on aggregate trends rather than individual patient targeting.
- **De-identification Best Practices**: Implementing multiple layers of data transformation to prevent re-identification of patient records.

The Future of RWD in Pharmaceutical Applications

The role of real-world data in pharmaceutical research and marketing continues evolving rapidly:

- **Integrated Data Sources**: Combining EHR information with claims databases, patient registries, and wearable device data provides increasingly comprehensive insights.
- **Advanced Analytics Implementation**: Sophisticated algorithms uncover previously unrecognized patterns within complex datasets, leading to more targeted development and marketing approaches.
- **Value-Based Focus**: Marketing increasingly emphasizes medications' comprehensive value propositions, including cost-effectiveness and improved patient outcomes in real-world settings.

Final Thoughts: The Future of EHR-Driven Marketing

As artificial intelligence, real-world evidence, and predictive analytics continue transforming healthcare marketing, success factors include:

- Ethical, patient-centered approaches that enhance treatment access and outcomes

- Transparent data practices that maintain provider and patient trust
- Regulatory compliance that adapts to evolving privacy protection requirements

What's Next?

In the next chapter, we will explore how EHRs can optimize patient engagement, including real-world examples of AI-powered outreach programs and evidence-based adherence initiatives.

PART TWO: LEVERAGING EHRs FOR STRATEGIC PHARMACEUTICAL MARKETING

Part Two

Leveraging EHRs for Strategic Pharmaceutical Marketing

This section will explore the multifaceted world of Electronic Health Records

The pharmaceutical landscape is undergoing a significant transformation. With the evolution of Electronic Health Records (EHRs) from simple digital repositories to sophisticated clinical tools, as explored in Part 1, the opportunities for precision marketing and enhanced patient engagement have expanded dramatically.

This section will explore how pharmaceutical companies can harness the power of EHRs to create data-driven marketing strategies that are both effective and ethically sound. We'll navigate the complex regulatory environment, examine practical approaches to patient engagement, and reveal strategies for crafting targeted messaging that resonates with healthcare providers and patients.

In Part 2, we will explore:

- **The Patient Engagement Revolution**: How EHRs are transforming the healthcare experience, enabling personalized communication, improved adherence, and better health outcomes. We'll examine real-world success stories and practical frameworks for implementing patient engagement strategies.
- **Navigating Regulatory Waters**: The intricate legal and ethical considerations surrounding the use of EHR data for marketing purposes. From HIPAA and GDPR to emerging AI regulations, we'll provide clear guidance for ensuring compliance while maintaining marketing effectiveness.
- **The Data-Driven Marketing Imperative**: How pharmaceutical companies can leverage EHR insights to develop sophisticated marketing approaches that enhance precision while respecting privacy boundaries. We'll explore frameworks for goal-setting, data source selection, and implementation of compliant workflows.

- **The Art and Science of Targeted Messaging**: Strategies for developing contextually relevant content that resonates with healthcare providers and patients. Through audience segmentation, channel optimization, and message development, we'll reveal how to create communications that drive engagement and results.

Throughout Part 2, we maintain a balanced perspective on the dual imperatives of marketing effectiveness and ethical responsibility. The most successful pharmaceutical organizations recognize that these objectives complement rather than contradict each other—building trust ultimately delivers superior business outcomes.

As we explore the intersection of EHRs and pharmaceutical marketing, we'll provide practical frameworks and actionable insights that can be implemented immediately. Whether you're a pharmaceutical marketer, healthcare executive, or technology leader, these chapters will equip you with the knowledge needed to navigate this complex but rewarding terrain.

By the end of Part 2, you will have a comprehensive understanding of how to leverage EHR data responsibly and effectively, creating value for all stakeholders in the healthcare ecosystem while advancing your organization's marketing objectives.

Chapter Five

Optimizing Patient Engagement Through EHRs

Introduction: Transforming Patient Experience Through Digital Engagement

For many patients, the healthcare journey is fragmented—characterized by missed follow-up appointments, complex medication regimens, and limited provider interactions. While previous chapters have explored how Electronic Health Records benefit providers and healthcare systems, this chapter focuses on their transformative potential for patients. Modern EHR systems now empower individuals with unprecedented access to their medical histories, streamlined appointment scheduling, and personalized health insights.

Despite these capabilities, many healthcare organizations struggle with low patient portal adoption rates, significantly limiting the potential impact of digital engagement tools. How can healthcare providers leverage EHR-driven strategies, AI-powered interventions, and engagement techniques like gamification to improve patient involvement, treatment adherence, and overall health outcomes?

This chapter explores:

- A compelling patient narrative illustrating the real-world impact of EHR portals
- The strategic role of artificial intelligence and digital engagement tools in enhancing treatment adherence
- Cleveland Clinic's innovative AI-powered patient engagement initiative
- How gamification principles improve patient motivation and treatment compliance
- A comprehensive strategy to increase patient portal adoption across diverse populations

A Patient's Journey: How an EHR Portal Changed Sarah's Life

Meet Sarah: A Chronic Disease Patient Who Struggled with Care Coordination

Sarah, a 58-year-old woman managing both type 2 diabetes and hypertension, faced multiple challenges:

- Inconsistent medication adherence—frequently forgetting to refill prescriptions on time
- Difficulty tracking laboratory results—often waiting days for updates from her healthcare providers
- Fragmented care coordination—seeing multiple specialists who weren't effectively aligned on her treatment plan

She frequently felt frustrated, overwhelmed, and disconnected from her own healthcare journey.

The Turning Point: Enrolling in an EHR-Integrated Patient Portal

Sarah's primary care physician introduced her to a mobile-friendly EHR portal that transformed her healthcare experience:

- Automated reminders for medication refills and upcoming appointments
- Immediate access to laboratory results, enabling her to track glucose and blood pressure trends over time
- A comprehensive shared care plan visible to all her providers—endocrinologist, cardiologist, and primary care physician
- AI-powered health coaching offering personalized dietary suggestions and lifestyle modifications based on her specific health data

The Outcome: Better Health, More Control

Within six months of active portal use, Sarah's clinical indicators showed significant improvement—her A1C levels decreased from 8.2% to 6.9%, her blood pressure stabilized within target range, and perhaps most importantly, she reported feeling significantly more confident in managing her health conditions.

Key Takeaway: Patient portals represent much more than digital record repositories—they empower individuals to take meaningful control of their health and well-being through improved access, communication, and engagement.

Case Study: Cleveland Clinic's AI-Powered Patient Engagement Strategy

The Challenge: Low Patient Engagement and Poor Adherence

Despite offering a fully functional EHR-integrated patient portal, Cleveland Clinic struggled with several critical challenges:

- Disappointing patient adoption rates (only 30% of eligible patients)
- Widespread medication non-adherence, leading to increased hospital readmissions
- Limited bidirectional digital communication between providers and patients

The Solution: AI-Powered Digital Patient Engagement

To address these persistent issues, Cleveland Clinic implemented a comprehensive strategy:

- AI-powered personalized reminders for medication adherence and follow-up appointments
- A thoroughly redesigned, mobile-optimized patient portal with enhanced user experience
- Intelligent chatbots for chronic disease management, delivering real-time health insights
- Condition-specific patient education resources automatically triggered by new diagnoses or significant laboratory results

The Outcome: Increased Engagement and Improved Health Outcomes

- Patient portal adoption increased dramatically from 30% to 72%
- Medication adherence improved by 45% among patients with chronic conditions
- Hospital readmissions decreased by 30%, with corresponding reductions in emergency department visits

Key Takeaway: Strategic EHR integration with intelligent engagement tools drives proactive patient participation, reducing long-term health risks while substantially improving treatment adherence.

The Role of Gamification and Mobile Apps in Patient Engagement

How Gamification Elements Help Patients

Gamification—the application of game design elements in non-game contexts—has emerged as a powerful approach in healthcare engagement. By incorporating features such as points, badges, leaderboards, and achievement challenges, gamification enhances patient motivation and treatment adherence. This section explores how these principles improve healthcare experiences and outcomes.

Enhancing Patient Engagement

Traditional healthcare approaches often struggle to maintain patient interest and participation. By introducing interactive game-like elements, providers create more engaging experiences. Mobile health applications that reward users with points for completing daily health tasks encourage patients to take active roles in their health management.

Increasing Motivation

Gamification significantly boosts patient motivation through visible rewards for positive behaviors. When patients earn badges for reaching milestones or compete on leaderboards with peers, they develop stronger commitment to health goals. This achievement recognition particularly benefits patients managing chronic conditions by reinforcing consistent adherence to treatment plans.

Promoting Treatment Adherence

As discussed in Chapter 4, treatment adherence represents a significant challenge in healthcare. Gamification improves adherence by transforming routine tasks into engaging activities. Patients receive medication or appointment reminders framed as game challenges, making these responsibilities feel less burdensome and more rewarding.

Fostering Social Connections

Many gamified health platforms include social features allowing users to share progress, participate in group challenges, or support others pursuing similar health goals. This community element provides emotional support and encouragement, reducing the isolation often experienced during health management.

Providing Immediate Feedback

Real-time feedback—a core gamification principle—enhances the patient experience by providing immediate responses to actions. When patients receive instant updates on progress, such as steps taken or medications taken on schedule, they can adjust behaviors accordingly. This feedback loop reinforces positive habits while quickly addressing potential issues.

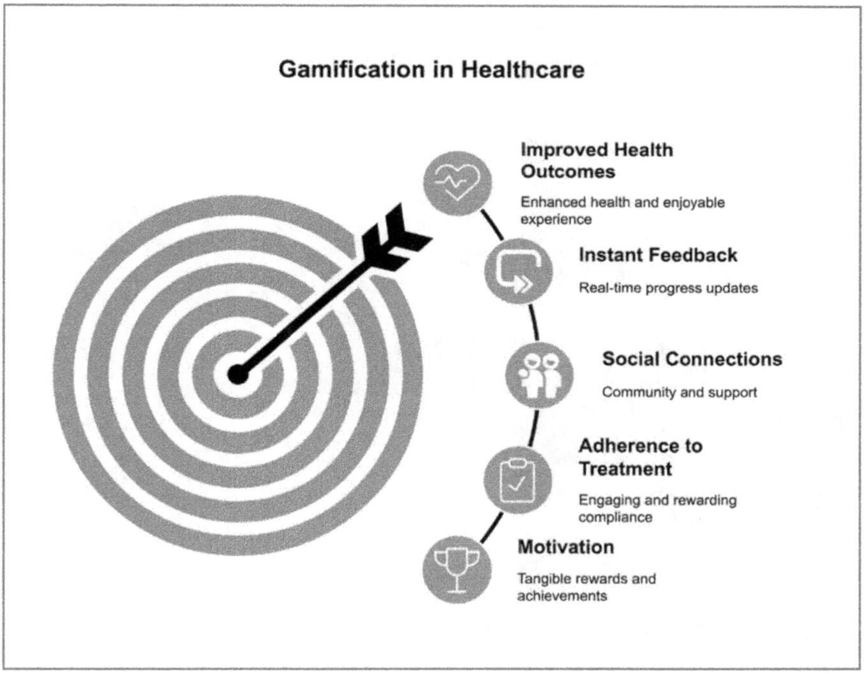

FIGURE 5.1: Gamification in Healthcare.

Integrating gamification into healthcare transforms patient experiences by enhancing engagement, motivation, adherence, social support, and feedback mechanisms. As healthcare continues evolving toward patient-centered approaches, these design principles create more effective and enjoyable health management experiences.

Key Takeaway: Gamification transforms health management from a series of obligations into an interactive, rewarding experience, significantly improving long-term patient engagement and outcomes.

How to Improve Patient Portal Adoption: A Step-by-Step Strategy

Many healthcare organizations struggle with suboptimal patient engagement in digital health platforms. Building on the EHR implementation principles discussed in Chapters 1 and 2, here is a proven strategy to improve adoption rates:

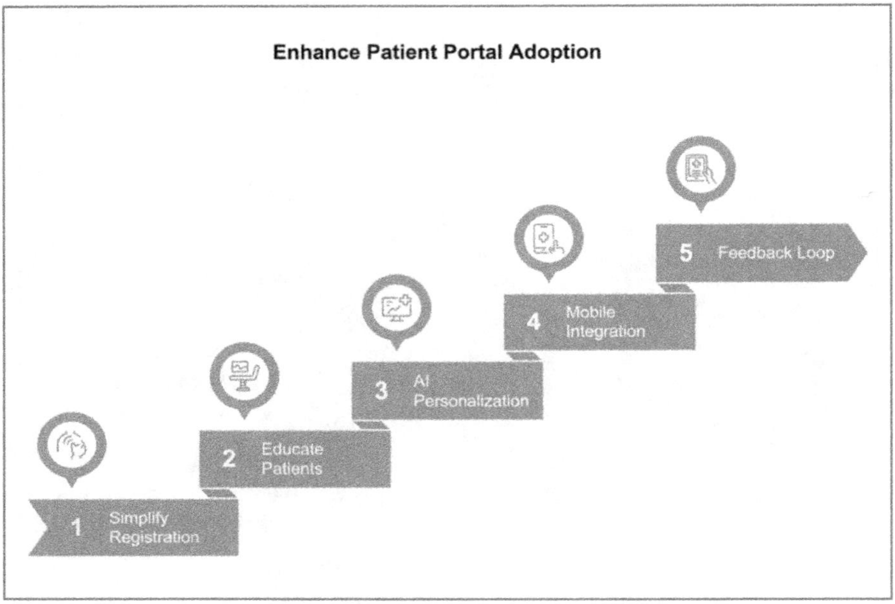

FIGURE 5.2: Enhancing Patient Portal Engagement.

Key Takeaway: A thoughtfully designed, user-friendly patient portal with AI-driven engagement features substantially increases adoption rates and supports sustained treatment adherence.

Final Thoughts: The Future of Patient Engagement Through EHRs

The future of patient engagement will increasingly emphasize personalized, interactive, and mobile-first experiences. Building on the security and privacy considerations outlined in Chapter 3, emerging trends include:

- Sophisticated AI-powered virtual health assistants providing real-time guidance and support
- Seamless integration of biometric data from wearable devices directly into EHR dashboards
- Predictive engagement modeling that identifies and addresses adherence risks before they manifest

Healthcare organizations that strategically embrace these innovations will lead in delivering patient-centered care that improves clinical outcomes while enhancing satisfaction and engagement.

What's Next?

In the following chapter, we will examine the regulatory landscape and ethical implications surrounding EHR data usage, ensuring both compliance and responsible innovation in leveraging technology for improved healthcare outcomes.

Chapter Six

Regulatory Considerations and Ethical Implications

Navigating Compliance in a Digital Healthcare Era

The growing integration of Electronic Health Records (EHRs) into healthcare systems brings tremendous opportunities alongside significant challenges. As explored in previous chapters, EHRs dramatically improve patient care, enable sophisticated pharmaceutical research, and enhance marketing precision. However, these benefits come with complex regulatory, ethical, and compliance considerations. Healthcare organizations must carefully balance data accessibility, security, and patient privacy within an increasingly stringent legal landscape.

This chapter explores:

- Key regulatory frameworks governing EHR data usage across global jurisdictions
- Emerging AI and data privacy regulations reshaping the healthcare industry
- A detailed case study on Google DeepMind's AI ethics challenges and lessons learned
- Common compliance pitfalls and strategic approaches to avoid them
- A comprehensive comparison of HIPAA, GDPR, and emerging AI healthcare regulations

Regulatory Considerations: The Evolving Landscape

Building on the security and privacy foundations outlined in Chapter 3, several key regulations govern healthcare technology utilization. The Health Insurance Portability and Accountability Act (HIPAA) remains the cornerstone of U.S. healthcare data protection, safeguarding patients' protected health information (PHI) through comprehensive national standards for electronic healthcare transactions and mandatory security measures.

The European Union's General Data Protection Regulation (GDPR) provides even more stringent requirements governing personal data processing, including health information. Unlike HIPAA's more limited scope, GDPR emphasizes transparency, individual control over personal data, and "privacy by design"—the principle that privacy protections must be integrated into technologies from their inception rather than added retroactively.

In the medical technology sphere, the Food and Drug Administration (FDA) regulates software applications and AI technologies used in healthcare settings. As EHR systems increasingly incorporate artificial intelligence capabilities discussed in earlier chapters, understanding these overlapping regulatory frameworks becomes essential for ensuring responsible implementation.

Ethical Implications: Beyond Regulatory Compliance

Regulatory compliance represents only the baseline for responsible EHR utilization. Equally important are the ethical considerations that should guide decision-making:

- **Data Ownership**: A fundamental question concerns who ultimately owns patient health data. Do patients themselves retain ownership rights, or do healthcare providers or technology companies have legitimate claims? This question influences everything from consent procedures to data monetization.
- **Informed Consent**: While obtaining patient consent for data usage is technically straightforward, ensuring patients truly understand the complexities of modern data analytics presents significant challenges. How can organizations ensure consent is genuinely informed in an era of sophisticated AI and predictive analytics?
- **Algorithmic Bias**: As discussed in Chapter 4, algorithms used in healthcare decision-making may unintentionally perpetuate or amplify societal biases. This can potentially lead to disparate outcomes across demographic groups, raising profound equity concerns.
- **Digital Divide**: Not all patients have equal access to technology or possess the digital literacy required to fully benefit from healthcare technology. Organizations must work diligently to bridge this gap to ensure the digital transformation of healthcare doesn't exacerbate existing disparities.

Examples of Regulatory Considerations in Practice

When healthcare organizations implement new EHR systems, they must navigate complex compliance requirements. A hospital deploying a new platform must ensure HIPAA compliance through robust security measures, established protocols for electronic transactions, and clear communication with patients about their privacy rights.

Mobile health applications often fall under FDA oversight, requiring developers to navigate complex regulatory guidelines based on the application's intended use and risk level. Cross-border telehealth services must simultaneously comply with multiple regulatory regimes, creating additional compliance challenges.

6.1 Understanding Regulations Governing EHR Data for Marketing Purposes

As explored in Chapter 4, Electronic Health Records contain valuable data that can inform pharmaceutical and healthcare marketing strategies. However, utilizing this information for marketing purposes raises specific regulatory concerns beyond those of general clinical use. This section examines the key regulations governing such applications.

HIPAA (Health Insurance Portability and Accountability Act)

The cornerstone of healthcare data privacy in the United States, HIPAA strictly regulates how Protected Health Information (PHI) can be used for marketing purposes:

- Marketing communications generally require specific patient authorization under HIPAA
- The law places substantial limitations on the sale of PHI
- HIPAA restricts the use of patient data for fundraising activities without proper consent

HITECH Act (Health Information Technology for Economic and Clinical Health Act)

This 2009 amendment to HIPAA further strengthened regulations regarding PHI used for marketing:

- It requires explicit written authorization from patients for disclosures serving marketing purposes

- This authorization must clearly state that the patient is permitting their data to be used specifically for marketing
- The Act significantly increased penalties for violations involving marketing misuse of patient data

Practical Application Examples

- A pharmaceutical company can only utilize EHR data from a healthcare system to identify patients with a specific condition and send targeted marketing materials if they have obtained proper written authorization
- A health insurance company cannot leverage patient data from EHRs to market additional insurance products without explicit consent from affected individuals

Nuances and Exceptions

HIPAA "Carve-outs": The law permits certain disclosures for what might appear to be marketing purposes without written authorizations, though these exceptions are narrowly defined:

- Healthcare providers can send patients reminders about preventive care screenings
- Organizations can distribute information about treatment options for patients' existing conditions

Direct-to-Consumer Marketing (DTCM): Regulations governing direct-to-consumer marketing utilizing EHR data are particularly complex:

- Companies marketing directly to consumers (e.g., weight loss programs) must navigate both HIPAA requirements and Federal Trade Commission (FTC) regulations concerning potentially deceptive marketing practices
- The regulatory landscape continues evolving as new marketing technologies emerge

International Considerations

GDPR (General Data Protection Regulation):

- The European Union's GDPR imposes significantly stricter regulations than HIPAA regarding data privacy
- Obtaining informed, specific consent for data use is paramount under GDPR

- GDPR includes a "right to be forgotten," allowing individuals to request deletion of their personal data

Looking Ahead: Technological Evolution

As data analytics and artificial intelligence capabilities continue developing, new challenges and opportunities regarding EHR data in marketing will emerge. For example, a company might develop an AI-powered platform analyzing anonymized patient data to identify disease prevalence trends, informing targeted public health campaigns without compromising individual privacy.

The regulations governing EHR data for marketing purposes strive to balance patient privacy protection with healthcare innovation. Understanding these evolving requirements is essential for any organization working with sensitive health information.

6.2 Balancing Marketing Goals with Patient Privacy and Ethical Considerations

As we explored marketing applications of EHR data in Chapter 4, this section examines how to balance legitimate marketing objectives with privacy protection and ethical responsibilities.

The Fundamental Challenge

- **Marketing Goals**: Reaching appropriate audiences with relevant healthcare information, promoting beneficial services and treatments, and fostering meaningful patient engagement
- **Patient Privacy Requirements**: Protecting sensitive health information as mandated by regulations like HIPAA and GDPR as discussed in Chapter 3
- **Ethical Considerations**: Building genuine patient trust, ensuring meaningful transparency in data usage, and avoiding exploitation or discrimination

Examples of Potential Conflicts

- **Targeted Advertising**: Using patient data to create precisely targeted social media advertisements promoting specific treatments might effectively reach relevant audiences but raises privacy concerns if not properly anonymized
- **Patient Testimonials**: Sharing authentic success stories with patient names and images can create compelling marketing content but requires explicit consent and careful protection of sensitive details

- **Advanced Data Analytics**: Leveraging patient data to identify trends and personalize marketing messages provides valuable insights but must be conducted using properly anonymized data and ethically sound methodologies

Case Study: Google DeepMind's AI Ethics Challenges

The Problem: Ethical Concerns in AI-Driven Healthcare

In 2017, Google DeepMind partnered with the United Kingdom's National Health Service (NHS) to develop an AI-powered system for early kidney disease detection. The initiative held tremendous potential for improving patient outcomes through earlier intervention. However, the partnership encountered significant regulatory challenges when investigators discovered that 1.6 million patient records had been accessed without obtaining proper consent as required under UK data protection laws and GDPR.

This controversy highlighted several critical concerns:

- Insufficient patient awareness and explicit consent in AI healthcare research
- Lack of transparency regarding how sensitive patient data would be utilized
- Potential risks associated with AI-driven diagnostics implemented without comprehensive ethical safeguards

How DeepMind Addressed Ethical and Regulatory Issues

Following public and regulatory backlash, DeepMind and the NHS implemented several corrective measures:

- Established stricter data governance policies preventing unauthorized data access
- Ensured all subsequent AI projects required explicit patient consent before accessing health records
- Developed transparent AI models allowing both clinicians and patients to understand the reasoning behind algorithmic decisions
- Created independent ethics review boards ensuring compliance with UK and EU regulations

The Results

- NHS and Google DeepMind comprehensively revised their data-sharing agreements to ensure GDPR compliance
- The organizations rebuilt patient trust, preventing additional regulatory penalties and potential litigation
- AI-driven healthcare innovation continued with enhanced oversight and accountability mechanisms

Contd...

Key Takeaways

- AI applications in healthcare must operate within clearly defined ethical and regulatory frameworks that prioritize patient rights
- Transparency in AI decision-making processes is essential for maintaining provider and patient trust
- Data-sharing agreements must comply with global privacy laws, particularly for cross-border AI collaborations

Strategies for Achieving Balance

- **Prioritize Patient Education**: Focus marketing efforts on educating patients about health conditions, treatment options, and preventive care. This approach builds trust and establishes expertise without compromising privacy.
- **Ensure Transparency and Obtain Informed Consent**: Be forthright with patients about how their data is collected, used, and protected. Obtain clear, unambiguous consent before using any patient data for marketing purposes.
- **Implement Granular Opt-in Options**: Give patients granular control over how their data is used. Provide clear opt-in and opt-out options for different types of marketing communications.
- **Build Trust as a Foundation**: Emphasize patient wellbeing and establish trust as the cornerstone of enduring patient relationships rather than pursuing short-term marketing advantages.

Examples of Balanced Approaches

- A healthcare system creates an educational blog series addressing chronic condition management. They use aggregate data to identify topics of interest but don't collect personal information from readers.
- A hospital develops a public health campaign promoting cancer screenings using anonymized data to highlight disease prevalence without disclosing any identifiable patient information.
- A provider enables patients to share experiences anonymously through carefully designed surveys, gathering valuable feedback while maintaining privacy.

Benefits of Strategic Balance

- **Enhanced Patient Trust**: Transparency and respect for privacy foster stronger patient-provider relationships
- **Ethical Brand Reputation**: Responsible marketing practices build positive organizational reputation
- **Improved Patient Outcomes**: Educational marketing empowers informed healthcare decisions
- **Sustainable Growth**: Organizations achieve lasting growth through patient loyalty built on trust

6.3 Building A Compliant and Responsible Approach to EHR-Based Marketing

Building on the marketing strategies discussed in Chapter 4 and the security frameworks outlined in Chapter 3, this section provides a comprehensive approach to compliant and responsible EHR-based marketing.

Understanding the Regulatory Foundation

- **HIPAA (Health Insurance Portability and Accountability Act)**: As previously discussed, HIPAA establishes the baseline for healthcare data privacy in the United States, with marketing disclosures generally requiring written patient authorization.
- **HITECH Act (Health Information Technology for Economic and Clinical Health Act)**: This amendment strengthened HIPAA's provisions specifically regarding marketing uses of protected health information.

Examples of Compliance in Practice

- A hospital can only utilize patient data from EHRs to target email campaigns about new services with proper written authorization
- A health insurance company cannot use patient data to market additional plans without explicit consent

Emerging Regulations: The Evolving Landscape

1. **The EU AI Act (2024 Proposal)**
   - Establishes a risk-based regulatory framework for AI applications in healthcare
   - Requires explainability and bias detection mechanisms in AI-driven diagnostic systems
   - Implements substantial penalties for AI misuse in patient care contexts
2. **The U.S. AI in Healthcare Regulatory Framework (Proposed 2025)**
   - Mandates transparency requirements for patient-facing healthcare applications
   - Strengthens FDA oversight of AI-driven diagnostic technologies
   - Requires continuous monitoring systems for AI-assisted clinical decision support
3. **The Global Health Data Protection Initiative (Planned 2026)**
   - Aims to standardize international patient data-sharing policies

- Introduces cross-border interoperability standards for AI-driven healthcare systems
- Establishes global frameworks for secure health information exchange

As these regulatory frameworks evolve, healthcare providers and technology companies must proactively align with emerging global compliance requirements.

Comparison of HIPAA, GDPR, and Emerging AI Healthcare Laws

Regulation	Region	Key Focus	Data Protection Measures	Impact on AI in EHRs
HIPAA (Health Insurance Portability and Accountability Act)	U.S.	Patient privacy & data security	Requires encryption, access controls, breach reporting	Limits AI access to de-identified health data
GDPR (General Data Protection Regulation)	EU	Data privacy & patient consent	Right to data access, deletion, and explicit consent	Mandates AI transparency and bias monitoring
EU AI Act (2024)	EU	AI risk management in healthcare	Requires explainability, bias detection, and human oversight	Applies strict controls on AI-driven EHR analysis
U.S. AI in Healthcare Framework (Proposed 2025)	U.S.	Regulating AI decision-making in medicine	Requires FDA approval for AI-assisted clinical tools	Strengthens oversight on AI-driven diagnostics
Global Health Data Protection Initiative (Planned 2026)	Inter-national	Standardizing cross-border health data exchange	Establishes international compliance frameworks	Creates global AI patient data standards

FIGURE 6.1: Comparison of HIPAA, GDPR, and Emerging AI Healthcare Laws.

By understanding these regulatory distinctions, healthcare organizations can ensure compliance while responsibly leveraging AI-driven innovations.

Beyond Compliance: Building a Comprehensive Responsible Approach

- **Patient Education Focus**: Prioritize creating marketing content that educates patients about health conditions, treatment options, and preventive care. This approach builds trust and provides value without compromising privacy.
- **Transparency and Informed Consent**: Communicate clearly with patients about data collection, usage, and protection practices. Obtain explicit consent before using patient data for marketing purposes and provide straightforward opt-out mechanisms.
- **Data Minimization and Anonymization**: Collect and utilize only essential data needed for specific marketing objectives. When using data for analytics, ensure comprehensive anonymization that eliminates personally identifiable information.
- **Ethical Segmentation and Targeting**: Leverage anonymized data to create appropriate audience segments based on demographic factors or general health needs while avoiding targeting based on sensitive health information.
- **Privacy-First Partnerships**: Never share patient data with third-party vendors for marketing purposes without explicit consent and thorough vetting of partner privacy practices.

Examples of Responsible Marketing Implementation

- A healthcare network creates condition-specific educational resources providing valuable information without collecting personal information from users.
- A hospital system develops a data-informed public health campaign promoting preventive screenings based on population-level insights, carefully avoiding any potentially identifiable patient information.
- A provider implements a targeted vaccination campaign using age and location data while meticulously avoiding usage of diagnostic or sensitive health information.

Benefits of a Comprehensive Responsible Approach

- **Strengthened Patient Trust**: Transparency and respect for privacy foster deeper patient relationships and higher engagement levels
- **Enhanced Reputation**: Ethical marketing practices build positive brand perception and patient loyalty
- **Improved Health Outcomes**: Educational marketing empowers informed healthcare decisions
- **Sustainable Organizational Growth**: Building trust through responsible practices creates lasting competitive advantage

Future Directions

- **Advanced Analytics Integration**: As AI and predictive analytics evolve, responsible adoption of these technologies will require ongoing ethical evaluation and governance
- **Patient-Centricity Evolution**: Healthcare marketing will increasingly emphasize personalized patient experiences while maintaining rigorous privacy protections

5 Common EHR Compliance Mistakes and How to Avoid Them

Organizations implementing EHR systems frequently encounter preventable compliance challenges. Here are five common mistakes and strategic approaches to address them:

1. **Inadequate Patient Consent Procedures**
   - **Mistake**: Failing to obtain properly documented patient consent before utilizing health data
   - **Solution**: Implement clear, specific opt-in mechanisms with comprehensive disclosure of data usage policies and regular consent refreshment
2. **Insufficient Data Security Measures**
   - **Mistake**: Deploying systems lacking robust encryption, multi-factor authentication, or intrusion detection capabilities

- **Solution**: Implement comprehensive cybersecurity frameworks with end-to-end encryption, continuous monitoring, and AI-powered threat detection as discussed in Chapter 3

3. **Limited Vendor Compliance Oversight**
   - **Mistake**: Inadequate verification that EHR vendors meet HIPAA, GDPR, or other applicable security standards
   - **Solution**: Require independent third-party security audits and formal compliance certifications from all vendors handling patient data
4. **Overpermissive Data Access Controls**
   - **Mistake**: Implementing excessive user access permissions that create unnecessary internal data exposure risks
   - **Solution**: Deploy granular role-based access controls (RBAC) limiting data access strictly to authorized personnel with legitimate need
5. **Non-Compliance with Emerging AI Regulations**
   - **Mistake**: Implementing AI-driven patient analytics without appropriate explainability features or bias detection mechanisms
   - **Solution**: Ensure all AI-enhanced EHR systems align with evolving regulatory requirements including GDPR, HIPAA, and emerging AI-specific healthcare laws

By proactively addressing these common pitfalls, healthcare organizations can significantly improve compliance posture, reduce legal exposure, and build stronger patient trust.

Final Thoughts: Preparing for the Future of EHR Compliance

As healthcare technology continues advancing rapidly, regulatory frameworks must evolve to maintain the delicate balance between innovation and patient rights protection. Forward-thinking organizations should:

- Adopt comprehensive ethical AI principles when implementing AI-enhanced EHR solutions
- Enhance patient transparency initiatives to build trust in increasingly data-driven healthcare models

- Proactively monitor global regulatory developments to ensure compliance across multiple jurisdictions

The future of effective EHR governance depends on meaningful collaboration between regulators, healthcare providers, technology developers, and patient advocates to create a secure, ethical, and genuinely patient-centered digital health ecosystem. By embracing both the letter and spirit of these evolving regulations, organizations can harness the transformative potential of EHR technology while maintaining the essential foundation of patient trust.

Chapter Seven

Data-Driven Marketing in Pharma

How EHR Data is Revolutionizing Pharma Marketing

The pharmaceutical industry has undergone a profound transformation—evolving from broad, mass-market campaigns to precision-targeted engagement strategies powered by Electronic Health Records (EHRs). As we explored in Chapters 4 and 5, data-driven marketing enables pharmaceutical companies to refine messaging, identify prescribing patterns, and optimize healthcare provider engagement with unprecedented accuracy. However, using patient data ethically while ensuring compliance with the global regulatory frameworks discussed in Chapter 6 remains a critical challenge for industry leaders.

This chapter explores:

- The transformative impact of EHR data on pharmaceutical marketing strategies
- Evidence-based case studies from Johnson & Johnson and Pfizer demonstrating measurable ROI
- Strategic approaches for sales teams to integrate EHR insights into healthcare provider outreach
- A comprehensive marketing compliance framework to ensure ethical engagement
- The emerging future of AI-powered pharmaceutical marketing initiatives

EHR Data for Marketing Insights: Balancing Innovation and Privacy

As discussed in Chapter 3, EHR data provides invaluable insights for marketing strategies, but its use is governed by stringent regulations like HIPAA. Building on our earlier exploration of data privacy, here's how pharmaceutical organizations can leverage EHR data responsibly:

- **Focus on De-identified Data**: Utilize thoroughly anonymized patient datasets that eliminate all personally identifiable information (PII) through robust technical safeguards.
- **Analyze Aggregate Trends**: Examine anonymized data in aggregate to identify patterns in demographics, diagnoses, or treatment approaches across defined patient populations.
- **Ensure Regulatory Compliance**: Verify all data collection, analysis, and marketing activities adhere to HIPAA requirements and additional relevant privacy laws as outlined in Chapter 6.

Examples of Ethically Using Anonymized EHR Data:

- A pharmaceutical company analyzes de-identified EHR data to identify geographic regions with higher prevalence of specific conditions, informing the development of targeted educational campaigns without compromising individual privacy.
- An oncology drug manufacturer examines anonymized treatment data to understand common side effect patterns, enabling the creation of more effective management protocols and patient education materials.

Developing a Patient-Centric Marketing Strategy

Building on the patient engagement principles discussed in Chapter 5, pharmaceutical marketers can leverage anonymized EHR insights to create patient-centered strategies with these key elements:

- **Targeted Content Development**: Create evidence-based educational materials across multiple channels (websites, blogs, social media) tailored to specific audience health profiles and information needs.

- **Strategic Audience Segmentation**: Segment audiences based on anonymized data insights to deliver personalized communications that resonate with specific healthcare concerns and treatment journeys.
- **Education-First Approach**: Prioritize educational content about health conditions, treatment options, and preventive measures to build credibility and trust while maintaining privacy boundaries.

Examples of Patient-Centric Pharmaceutical Marketing:

- A diabetes medication manufacturer develops a series of condition management resources based on anonymized EHR insights about common adherence challenges and complications.
- A pharmaceutical company creates a targeted awareness campaign about an underdiagnosed condition, using de-identified prevalence data to reach appropriate audiences with educational content.

Performance Measurement Framework

Metric Category	Key Performance Indicators	Measurement Tools	Strategic Value
Engagement	Website traffic, content interaction rates, time spent with materials	Web analytics, CRM systems	Indicates content relevance and resonance
Conversion	Information requests, physician discussions, prescription initiations	Campaign tracking, physician surveys	Measures practical impact on treatment decisions
Education Impact	Knowledge improvement, behavior change intentions	Pre/post assessments, longitudinal studies	Evaluates true educational effectiveness
Long-term Outcomes	Medication adherence, health outcomes, patient satisfaction	De-identified prescription data, outcomes research	Demonstrates ultimate value proposition

FIGURE 7.1: Comprehensive Pharmaceutical Marketing Measurement Framework.

The Future of Data-Driven Pharmaceutical Marketing

- **Advanced Analytics Integration**: As artificial intelligence and machine learning capabilities advance, pharmaceutical marketers will gain deeper insights from anonymized EHR data, enabling increasingly personalized communications and improved engagement strategies.
- **Enhanced Patient Experience Focus**: The evolution of pharmaceutical marketing will emphasize creating seamless patient experiences through the treatment journey. Data-driven insights can inform strategies to improve education, support adherence, and enhance overall satisfaction.

Developing comprehensive data-driven marketing strategies with EHR insights empowers pharmaceutical organizations to reach the right providers and patients with appropriate messaging at optimal times. However, as emphasized throughout this book, prioritizing patient privacy, utilizing anonymized data ethically, and focusing on valuable educational content remain essential principles for responsible marketing practices.

Case Study: How Johnson & Johnson Trained Marketers to Use EHR Data

The Challenge: Data Literacy Gaps in Marketing Teams

Johnson & Johnson identified a significant gap in their marketing organization: despite substantial investments in data infrastructure, marketing teams weren't effectively utilizing EHR-driven insights to refine their outreach strategies. Traditional marketing approaches relied heavily on sales representative observations and general prescribing patterns, resulting in suboptimal healthcare provider targeting and engagement.

Johnson & Johnson's EHR Data Training Initiative

To address this capability gap, Johnson & Johnson implemented a comprehensive six-month training program for marketing teams that included:

- **AI & EHR Data Interpretation Workshops**: Specialized training modules teaching marketers how to interpret complex prescribing trends and identify meaningful patterns.
- **Hands-on Analytics Training**: Practical sessions enabling teams to work directly with anonymized real-world datasets to develop targeting strategies.

Contd..

- **Cross-Functional Collaboration Programs**: Structured initiatives aligning marketing teams with data science experts, compliance specialists, and field sales representatives.

Measurable Results

The training initiative delivered substantial business impact:

- 85% of marketing team members achieved proficiency in EHR-driven analytics applications
- 30% improvement in healthcare provider targeting precision, resulting in measurably higher engagement rates
- Significantly enhanced regulatory compliance, reducing risks associated with improper data utilization

Key Implementation Insights

- Pharmaceutical marketing teams require specialized training in healthcare data analytics to maximize outreach effectiveness
- AI-driven insights substantially enhance ROI and compliance when implemented with appropriate ethical safeguards
- Cross-functional collaboration ensures proper data governance and more effective marketing decision-making

Source: Johnson & Johnson Digital Marketing Strategy Report (2022)

7.1 Setting Goals and Objectives for EHR-Based Marketing Initiatives

Aligning Strategy with Measurable Outcomes

Leveraging EHR data for pharmaceutical marketing requires establishing clear, measurable objectives. The SMART framework provides a structured approach to goal-setting, ensuring initiatives are:

- **Specific**: Clearly defining exact outcomes the campaign aims to achieve
- **Measurable**: Establishing concrete metrics to track progress toward objectives
- **Attainable**: Setting realistic targets achievable with available resources
- **Relevant**: Ensuring alignment with broader marketing strategy and organizational priorities
- **Time-bound**: Defining specific timeframes for achieving each objective

Examples of SMART Goals in HER Based Marketing

Goal 1: Increase healthcare provider awareness of a new treatment option for rheumatoid arthritis by leveraging EHR-derived insights.

Supporting Objectives:

- **Specific**: Develop and launch a targeted educational campaign for rheumatologists who frequently treat moderate-to-severe rheumatoid arthritis patients.
- **Measurable**: Increase specialist awareness of the treatment's efficacy profile by 40% (measured through pre/post surveys) within six months of campaign launch.
- **Attainable**: Based on previous educational initiatives and available channels, this awareness increase is realistic.
- **Relevant**: This objective directly supports the broader goal of increasing appropriate treatment adoption.
- **Time-bound**: Complete the initial awareness phase within six months, with quarterly measurement points.

Goal 2: Improve medication adherence for patients prescribed the company's cardiovascular therapy.

Supporting Objectives:

- **Specific**: Develop personalized educational resources for patients newly prescribed the cardiovascular medication, addressing common adherence barriers identified through anonymized EHR data analysis.
- **Measurable**: Increase 90-day medication adherence rates by 25% compared to historical benchmarks.
- **Attainable**: Similar adherence programs have demonstrated improvements in this range.
- **Relevant**: Enhancing adherence aligns with both improved patient outcomes and business objectives.
- **Time-bound**: Measure impact over a 12-month period following program implementation.

Beyond SMART Goals: Ethical Considerations

- **Education Priority**: Goals should emphasize providing valuable information rather than simply driving prescription volume.
- **Regulatory Alignment**: Ensure all objectives comply with relevant regulations discussed in Chapter 6.

- **Patient-Centered Outcomes**: Incorporate metrics focused on improved patient wellbeing and health literacy.

Example: ***Goal***: Enhance patient understanding of medication adherence importance for chronic condition management.

Objective: Develop and distribute targeted educational content through approved channels, measuring knowledge improvement through voluntary assessments.

7.2 Identifying the Right Data Sources and Analytics Tools Building a Strong Analytical Foundation

EHRs contain valuable patient information, but extracting actionable marketing insights requires appropriate tools and data sources. This section explores how to identify the most suitable resources for pharmaceutical marketing initiatives while maintaining the privacy protections discussed in Chapter 3.

Strategic Data Sources

Pharmaceutical marketers should consider two primary categories of data:

1. **Internal EHR Data**: This represents the most relevant information source, containing detailed patient demographics, diagnoses, medications, and treatment histories. As emphasized in Chapter 6, strict regulations govern its use:
    - Must be properly de-identified according to HIPAA standards
    - Requires appropriate data use agreements and governance processes
    - Often accessed through healthcare partners rather than directly
2. **Complementary External Sources**: Public health statistics, demographic information, and market research can provide additional context:
    - Claims databases offer insights into treatment patterns and medication utilization
    - Social determinants of health data provide contextual understanding of patient populations
    - Published research literature validates patterns observed in EHR data

Privacy and Ethical Imperatives

- **Prioritize De-identification**: Always ensure robust anonymization of patient data through established technical methods.
- **Analyze Aggregate Trends**: Focus on population-level patterns rather than individual-level insights.

- **Maintain Regulatory Compliance**: Verify all data acquisition and utilization adheres to relevant privacy regulations.

Analytics Tool Selection Framework

Tool Category	Appropriate Applications	Key Considerations	Example Solutions
Spreadsheet Applications	Basic analysis of limited datasets	Limited for complex analysis, Privacy concerns with local storage	Microsoft Excel, Google Sheets
Business Intelligence Platforms	Visual dashboards, Trend reporting, Pattern identification	User-friendly interfaces, Stronger visualization capabilities	Tableau, Microsoft Power BI, Qlik
Data Warehousing Solutions	Enterprise-scale data integration, Complex dataset management	Technical expertise required, Higher implementation costs	Amazon Redshift, Google BigQuery, Snowflake
Healthcare-Specific Analytics	Purpose-built healthcare analysis, Regulatory compliance features	Industry-specific capabilities, Pre-built healthcare models	IBM Watson Health, SAS Healthcare Analytics, Health Catalyst
Advanced AI/ML Platforms	Predictive modeling, Natural language processing, Pattern discovery	Significant expertise required, Comprehensive governance needed	DataRobot, H2O.ai, Dataiku

FIGURE 7.2: Analytics Tool Selection Framework for Pharmaceutical Marketing.

Implementation Scenarios

Scenario 1: A mid-sized pharmaceutical company wants to understand treatment patterns for a chronic condition to better target educational outreach.

- **Appropriate Solution**: A business intelligence platform like Tableau connected to de-identified EHR data could provide sufficient visualization and pattern recognition capabilities.

Scenario 2: A large pharmaceutical manufacturer needs to analyze complex relationships between multiple treatment approaches, outcomes, and patient characteristics across diverse populations.

- **Appropriate Solution**: An advanced analytics platform with machine learning capabilities, potentially combined with healthcare-specific analytics tools, would provide the necessary depth of analysis.

Critical Selection Factors

- **Data Security**: Select tools with robust security features aligned with healthcare compliance requirements.
- **Usability**: Choose solutions appropriate for your team's technical expertise level.
- **Scalability**: Consider future analytical needs and growth in data volume.
- **Compliance Features**: Prioritize tools with built-in compliance capabilities for healthcare data.

7.3 Building A Compliant Workflow for Accessing and Utilizing EHR Data

Safeguarding Privacy While Ensuring Marketing Effectiveness

Building on the security frameworks outlined in Chapter 3 and the regulatory considerations from Chapter 6, pharmaceutical companies must implement structured processes for EHR data utilization. Here's a comprehensive approach to building compliant workflows:

1. **Define Granular Access Controls**
    - Identify specific use cases and data requirements for each marketing initiative
    - Establish a clear hierarchy of authorized users with role-appropriate permissions
    - Implement role-based access controls (RBAC) within data systems to enforce permissions

    Example: Marketing analytics teams might access de-identified, aggregated data for trend analysis, while only specific research personnel with appropriate training can access more detailed anonymized datasets.

2. **Implement Data Minimization Principles**
    - Access only the minimum data elements necessary for specific marketing objectives

- Apply robust anonymization techniques to eliminate personally identifiable information
- Document justification for each data element utilized in marketing analyses

Example: When analyzing treatment patterns for a specific condition, limit data extraction to relevant diagnostic codes, anonymized prescription information, and basic demographic categories rather than comprehensive patient records.

Pharmaceutical Marketing Data Governance Workflow

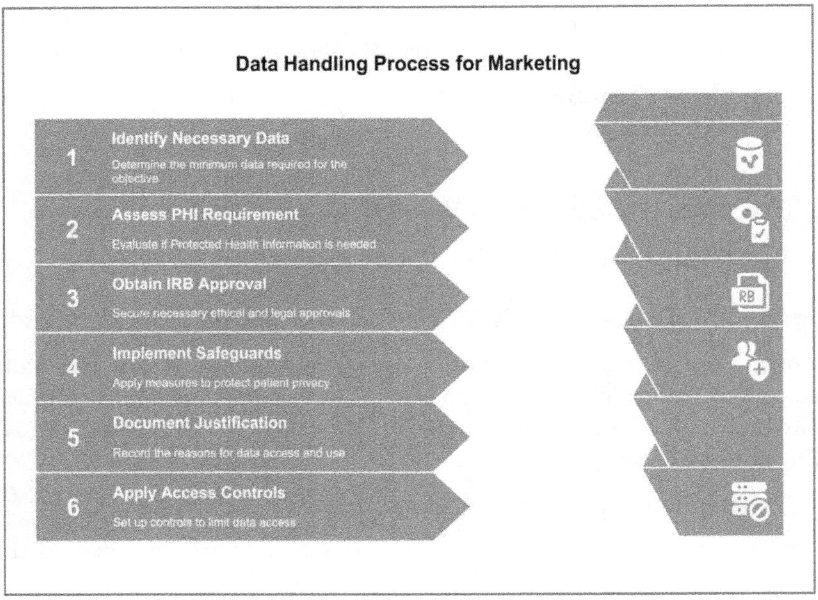

FIGURE 7.3: Compliant Pharmaceutical Marketing Data Workflow.

3. **Establish Comprehensive Security Protocols**
   - Deploy end-to-end encryption for all sensitive data both at rest and in transit
   - Implement multi-factor authentication for accessing EHR-derived marketing datasets
   - Conduct regular security assessments and penetration testing of marketing data environments

Example: Require biometric verification in addition to strong passwords for accessing marketing analytics platforms containing healthcare data, with automatic session timeouts after periods of inactivity.

4. **Manage Patient Consent Appropriately**
   - Understand when written patient authorization is required under HIPAA for specific marketing activities
   - Develop clear, understandable consent documentation explaining data usage when required
   - Maintain systems for tracking consent status and honoring opt-out requests

   Example: When developing patient support programs based on identifiable patient information, implement a robust consent management system that documents authorization and enables immediate opt-out processing.

5. **Maintain Comprehensive Audit Trails**
   - Record all data access activities with user identification, timestamp, and purpose
   - Document specific data elements accessed for each marketing initiative
   - Conduct regular audit reviews to identify potential compliance issues

   Example: Generate weekly reports of all marketing analytics data access, including which team members accessed what information and for which approved campaigns.

6. **Integrate with Compliant Marketing Systems**
   - Select marketing automation platforms with built-in HIPAA compliance capabilities
   - Verify vendor compliance through security assessments and BAA agreements
   - Establish secure data transfer protocols between systems

   Example: When implementing CRM solutions for pharmaceutical sales teams, select platforms with healthcare-specific compliance features and documentation capabilities.

7. **Provide Ongoing Education and Training**
   - Conduct regular training on healthcare privacy regulations for all marketing personnel
   - Develop clear guidelines for appropriate use of EHR-derived insights
   - Create escalation paths for addressing potential compliance questions

Example: Implement quarterly privacy training sessions for marketing teams with scenario-based exercises addressing common compliance challenges in pharmaceutical marketing.

Best Practices for Ethical & Compliant Pharma Marketing

Marketing Compliance Checklist

To ensure ethical engagement while leveraging EHR data, pharmaceutical companies should adhere to these best practices:

Compliance Domain	Key Requirements	Implementation Actions
Data Anonymization	• Remove all identifiers from patient data • Ensure statistical techniques prevent re-identification • Validate anonymization effectiveness	• Work exclusively with properly de-identified data • Implement technical safeguards exceeding minimum requirements • Conduct regular re-identification risk assessments
Educational Focus	• Prioritize scientific accuracy in all content • Ensure balanced presentation of benefits and risks • Provide context for appropriate use	• Develop evidence-based educational materials • Ensure medical/legal review of all content • Maintain clear separation between education and promotion
Regulatory Alignment	• Comply with all applicable regulations • Maintain documentation of compliance efforts • Stay current with evolving requirements	• Partner with compliant data vendors • Conduct regular compliance audits • Implement governance committees for oversight
Ethical AI Implementation	• Prevent algorithmic bias in targeting • Maintain human oversight of AI systems • Ensure transparency in AI applications	• Test AI models with diverse datasets • Implement regular bias audits • Document AI decision factors

FIGURE 7.4: Pharmaceutical Marketing Compliance Framework.

By following these structured best practices, pharmaceutical marketers can maximize engagement effectiveness while maintaining ethical standards and regulatory compliance.

Case Study: How Pfizer Used AI & EHR Data for Targeted Oncology Marketing

The Challenge: Inefficient Healthcare Provider Outreach

Pfizer encountered significant challenges in effectively engaging oncologists for a newly approved targeted cancer therapy. Traditional marketing approaches—including sales representative visits and general awareness campaigns—failed to reach the most appropriate physicians with relevant information at optimal moments in the treatment decision process.

Pfizer's AI-Enhanced, EHR-Driven Precision Targeting

Pfizer partnered with specialized EHR data analytics firms to implement a multi-faceted approach:

- **Prescribing Pattern Analysis**: Using anonymized EHR data to identify oncologists most likely to treat patients matching the therapy's indication profile
- **AI-Powered Patient Cohort Modeling**: Leveraging machine learning to detect patterns in de-identified patient records that matched the drug's ideal candidate profile
- **EHR Workflow Integration**: Developing clinical decision support tools providing educational materials at relevant points in the oncologist's workflow

Measurable Results

The initiative delivered significant performance improvements:

- 35% increase in appropriate oncologist adoption within the first year
- 25% reduction in marketing expenditure through more precise physician targeting
- Substantial improvement in physician confidence regarding appropriate patient selection

Strategic Implementation Insights

- EHR-informed analytics dramatically improve healthcare provider targeting precision, enhancing cost-effectiveness
- AI-powered insights enable more contextually relevant engagement with specialists
- Integrating educational content directly into clinical workflows increases awareness and appropriate utilization

Source: Pfizer AI-Powered HCP Engagement Report (2022)

HCP Engagement Strategies: Integrating EHR Data in Outreach

How Sales Teams Can Leverage EHR Data More Effectively

Building on the patient engagement principles discussed in Chapter 5, pharmaceutical sales and marketing teams can implement these evidence-based strategies:

1. **Analyze Predictive Prescribing Patterns**
   - Use anonymized EHR analytics to identify physicians who regularly treat relevant patient populations
   - Focus engagement efforts on providers most likely to consider appropriate new treatment options
   - Develop territory strategies based on data-driven insights rather than traditional geographic boundaries
2. **Implement AI-Enhanced Personalized Messaging**
   - Deliver precisely relevant educational content based on a healthcare provider's patient population and practice patterns
   - Leverage AI-driven segmentation to refine communication approaches for different provider types
   - Customize messaging timing based on identified practice workflows and decision points
3. **Integrate Educational Content Within EHR Systems**
   - Develop clinical decision support tools providing relevant information at appropriate moments
   - Incorporate clinical trial data, safety updates, and prescribing guidance within existing clinical workflows
   - Design non-disruptive notifications that respect the provider's time and attention

Healthcare Provider Engagement Model

By implementing these strategic approaches, pharmaceutical sales teams can significantly improve healthcare provider engagement while maintaining appropriate ethical boundaries and providing genuine value.

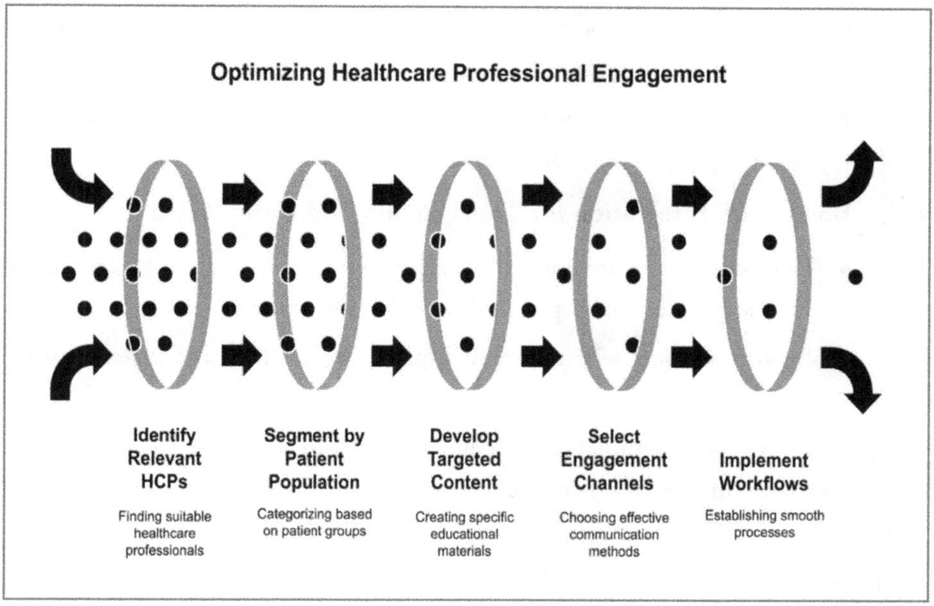

FIGURE 7.5: Data-Driven HCP Engagement Cycle.

The Future of AI-Powered Pharma Marketing

The integration of artificial intelligence with EHR data is rapidly transforming pharmaceutical marketing. These emerging trends will reshape industry practices:

1. **Hyper-Personalized HCP Engagement**
    - Advanced AI systems will enable truly real-time healthcare provider engagement
    - Natural language processing will analyze scientific communications to identify emerging treatment patterns
    - Predictive analytics will optimize messaging timing, content, and channel selection for maximum relevance
2. **AI-Enhanced Patient Journey Analysis**
    - Pharmaceutical companies will leverage longitudinal anonymized EHR data to develop more effective adherence support programs

- AI algorithms will identify specific adherence risk factors and optimize intervention timing
- Machine learning models will detect subtle patterns in treatment journeys, improving educational resource development

3. **Blockchain Integration for Transparency and Compliance**
   - Blockchain technology will create immutable records of marketing interactions, enhancing compliance documentation
   - Smart contracts will automate appropriate use limitations for sensitive healthcare data
   - AI-powered compliance monitoring will provide real-time guidance to maintain regulatory adherence

As artificial intelligence and machine learning capabilities continue evolving, EHR-driven pharmaceutical marketing will become increasingly precise, ethical, and effective—improving healthcare provider engagement while enhancing patient outcomes through better treatment decisions.

Final Thoughts: Ethical, Data-Driven Pharmaceutical Engagement

By thoughtfully integrating artificial intelligence, EHR data analytics, and predictive modeling, pharmaceutical companies can:

- Significantly enhance targeted healthcare provider outreach while maintaining rigorous compliance
- Improve patient outcomes by supporting more informed treatment selection and adherence
- Build enduring trust through ethical, education-focused marketing approaches

Organizations that embrace responsible data utilization while implementing the strategic frameworks outlined in this chapter will lead the next generation of pharmaceutical engagement—creating value for healthcare providers, patients, and the healthcare system as a whole.

Chapter Eight

Crafting Targeted Messaging Using EHR Data

The Role of EHR Data in Personalized Pharma Communication

As pharmaceutical companies continue their transition to data-driven marketing strategies discussed in Chapter 7, the ability to deliver precisely targeted, contextually relevant, and clinically impactful messaging has become increasingly critical. Electronic Health Record insights enable a new level of precision engagement, ensuring healthcare providers and patients receive information specifically aligned with their treatment needs and clinical contexts. However, as emphasized in Chapters 3 and 6, ethical considerations and regulatory compliance remain foundational to any approach utilizing sensitive healthcare data.

This chapter explores:

- How EHR-derived insights fundamentally reshape pharmaceutical communication strategies
- Evidence-based case studies demonstrating successful applications of targeted messaging
- Best practices for implementing personalized, non-intrusive engagement approaches
- Practical frameworks for ensuring ethical and regulatory-compliant messaging

Leveraging EHR Insights for Strategic Messaging

As explored in previous chapters, Electronic Health Records contain extraordinarily valuable patient information that—when properly de-identified and ethically utilized—can inform highly targeted marketing communications. Building on the data governance principles established in Chapter 7, this section examines how to transform EHR insights into effective messaging strategies.

Uncovering Actionable Patient Insights

When appropriately anonymized and analyzed according to the privacy frameworks discussed in Chapters 3 and 6, EHR data reveals critical patterns that can inform messaging strategy:

- **Population Demographics**: Comprehensive understanding of patient characteristics including age distribution, geographic concentration, and relevant socioeconomic factors
- **Clinical Conditions**: Identification of prevalent diagnoses and comorbidities within specific patient populations
- **Treatment Trajectories**: Insights into common treatment pathways, medication utilization patterns, and therapy sequencing

Examples of Insight Application

- A large healthcare network analyzes de-identified EHR data and discovers significantly higher prevalence of uncontrolled asthma among pediatric populations in specific underserved communities
- A pharmaceutical manufacturer identifies treatment adherence challenges in patients with complex chronic conditions through anonymized longitudinal data analysis

Transforming Data Insights into Strategic Messaging

Once meaningful patterns have been identified through appropriate data analysis, pharmaceutical marketers can develop highly targeted communications that address specific needs:

- **Strategic Segmentation**: Divide target audiences into meaningful subgroups based on anonymized clinical characteristics, practice patterns, or treatment approaches
- **Content Customization**: Develop specialized educational materials tailored to each segment's specific information needs and clinical contexts
- **Educational Prioritization**: Focus on delivering genuinely valuable clinical information rather than promotional messaging

Examples of Targeted Messaging Implementation

- Using insights about pediatric asthma prevalence, a pharmaceutical company develops a healthcare provider education campaign focusing on identifying undertreated patients and addressing specific environmental triggers common in identified communities

- Based on adherence data, a manufacturer creates targeted educational resources addressing identified medication management challenges for patients with multiple chronic conditions

Looking Beyond Traditional Segmentation Variables

While demographic factors and clinical diagnoses provide foundational insights, sophisticated messaging strategies incorporate additional dimensions:

- **Provider Interest Patterns**: Analyzing engagement with scientific content to understand specific clinical interests beyond specialty designation
- **Practice Context**: Considering factors like practice setting, patient population characteristics, and resource constraints
- **Decision-Making Styles**: Recognizing differences in how healthcare providers evaluate and implement new treatment approaches

Examples of Multidimensional Segmentation

- A specialty pharmaceutical company develops tailored content for community oncologists who frequently refer patients to academic medical centers, addressing their specific information needs around pre-referral workup and ongoing co-management
- A digital health platform creates targeted messaging for providers who demonstrate particular interest in emerging clinical guidelines based on their engagement with relevant medical literature

Principles of Effective Healthcare Messaging

Regardless of audience segment, several core principles enhance message effectiveness:

- **Focus on Patient Outcomes**: Emphasize how therapeutic approaches improve meaningful clinical outcomes rather than product features
- **Use Precise, Accessible Language**: Balance scientific accuracy with clarity, avoiding unnecessary jargon while maintaining clinical credibility
- **Demonstrate Clinical Empathy**: Acknowledge the challenges providers and patients face within the healthcare system

Message Development Framework

Message Element	Key Considerations	Example Implementation
Core Clinical Message	• Evidence-based information • Clinically meaningful outcomes • Appropriate context	"For appropriate patients with moderate-to-severe disease, Treatment X demonstrated a 42% reduction in symptom severity in clinical trials"
Value Proposition	• Patient-centered benefits • Health system considerations • Quality of life impact	"Treatment X's once-monthly dosing may improve adherence while reducing administration burden for patients with multiple therapies"
Supporting Evidence	• Relevant clinical data • Real-world outcomes • Appropriate limitations	"In the Phase III LANDMARK study (n=842), patients achieved significant symptom improvement by week 4, maintained through 52 weeks"
Next Steps	• Clear, specific actions • Resource accessibility • Follow-up pathways	"Download our patient identification checklist or schedule a consultation with our clinical educator to discuss appropriate patient selection"

FIGURE 8.1: Clinical Message Development Framework.

How EHR Data Enhances Targeted Communication

Building on the data analytics approaches discussed in Chapter 7, EHR insights enable several advanced communication strategies:

1. **Real-Time Clinical Decision Support (CDS)**
    - Contextually relevant educational materials embedded within healthcare provider workflows at key clinical decision points
    - Timely delivery of safety information, prescribing guidelines, and appropriate patient selection criteria
    - Non-disruptive integration within existing clinical processes to respect provider time constraints

2. **AI-Enhanced Healthcare Provider Segmentation**
   - Identification of specialists and high-volume prescribers most relevant to specific therapeutic areas
   - Predictive modeling to anticipate provider interest in emerging treatment approaches
   - Pattern recognition to identify early adopters and clinical opinion leaders
3. **Behavioral Insights for Message Optimization**
   - Customization of content based on observed prescribing patterns and treatment preferences
   - Strategic adjustment of message frequency and channel selection based on engagement analytics
   - Continuous refinement through feedback and response analysis
4. **Patient Support Communication Systems**
   - Timely adherence reminders and education based on prescription fulfillment patterns
   - Condition-specific educational content delivery aligned with treatment milestones
   - Supportive messaging addressing known adherence barriers identified through anonymized patient data

Communication Channel Selection Matrix

Channel	Strengths	Limitations	Ideal Applications
EHR-Integrated Messaging	• Workflow integration • Point-of-care relevance • Clinical context	• Implementation complexity • System variability • Technical constraints	• Clinical decision support • Safety updates • Formulary information
Email Communication	• Detailed content delivery • Trackable engagement • Resource efficiency	• Inbox competition • Deliverability challenges • Format limitations	• Clinical updates • Educational content • Program announce-ments

Contd...

Channel	Strengths	Limitations	Ideal Applications
Digital Detailing	• Interactive capabilities • Visual presentation • Personalized delivery	• Scheduling constraints • Technology requirements • Higher cost	• New product information • Complex messaging • Visual data presentation
SMS/Mobile Messaging	• Immediate delivery • High visibility • Brief interactions	• Length limitations • Format constraints • Regulatory considerations	• Brief updates • Reminders • Resource links
Social Media Platforms	• Community engagement • Content sharing • Broader reach	• Control limitations • Regulatory complexity • Message consistency	• Disease awareness • Thought leadership • Community building

FIGURE 8.2: Healthcare Communication Channel Selection Matrix.

Case Study: Doceree's Trigger-Based Messaging Enhances Lupus Therapy Prescriptions

The Challenge: Limited Awareness of Coverage & Patient Support Programs

A pharmaceutical manufacturer sought to increase appropriate prescriptions for a biologic lupus therapy by ensuring healthcare providers had timely access to formulary coverage information and co-pay assistance program details. Traditional outreach approaches—including standard emails and field force visits—proved insufficient in engaging providers at the critical moment of treatment decision-making.

Strategic Solution: EHR-Integrated Contextual Messaging

By implementing Doceree's AI-powered EHR messaging platform, the company developed a sophisticated trigger-based messaging approach to:

- Deliver precisely relevant formulary and financial support information within the EHR system at the exact moment of prescribing consideration
- Ensure providers received comprehensive support program details during actual treatment selection

Contd...

- Reduce financial barriers to appropriate therapy by improving provider awareness of affordability resources

Measurable Outcomes

The initiative delivered significant clinical and business impact:

- 19% increase in appropriate prescriptions for the biologic therapy
- Substantially improved healthcare provider awareness of coverage details and patient support resources
- Enhanced medication adherence through improved affordability and comprehensive support

Key Implementation Insights

- EHR-integrated messaging delivers information precisely when it influences clinical decisions
- Contextual approaches addressing specific barriers (like affordability concerns) can significantly impact appropriate therapy utilization
- AI-powered targeting can optimize engagement effectiveness while maintaining regulatory compliance

Source: Doceree's Case Study on EHR Messaging for Lupus Therapy (2022)

8.1 Segmentation Strategies Based on Patient Demographics and Treatment History

From Broad Categories to Precision Segments

Building on the data-driven marketing approaches introduced in Chapter 7, pharmaceutical marketers can implement sophisticated segmentation strategies using anonymized EHR insights. Moving beyond traditional demographic segmentation, these approaches enable truly personalized communication aligned with specific clinical needs.

Demographic Segmentation Enhancement

While basic demographic factors provide a foundation, EHR insights enable more nuanced understanding:

- **Age-Related Clinical Patterns**: Rather than basic age groupings, identify specific age-related clinical patterns, such as early-onset disease presentations or geriatric-specific treatment considerations
- **Geographic Clinical Variations**: Recognize regional differences in disease prevalence, treatment approaches, and healthcare resource utilization

- **Social Determinants Context**: Incorporate understanding of how social determinants of health impact treatment access, adherence, and outcomes

Treatment History Segmentation

EHR-derived insights enable particularly sophisticated segmentation based on clinical history patterns:

- **Diagnostic Journey Analysis**: Segment patients and providers based on diagnostic pathways, identifying opportunities for earlier intervention or diagnosis
- **Treatment Response Patterns**: Recognize variations in therapy response across different patient populations to enable more personalized approaches
- **Medication Utilization Insights**: Understand actual medication usage patterns, including adherence challenges, switching behaviors, and combination therapies

Advanced Segmentation Framework

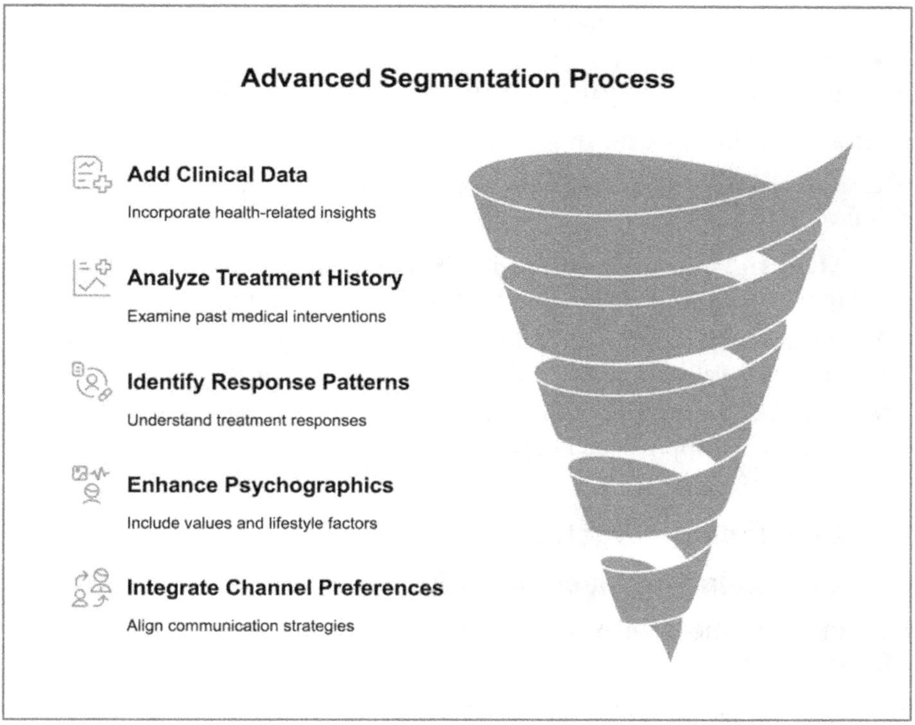

FIGURE 8.3: Progressive Segmentation Development Process.

Integrated Segmentation Approach

The most effective segmentation strategies combine multiple dimensions to create truly meaningful audience groups:

- **Clinical Presentation + Treatment History**: Targeting healthcare providers who treat patients with specific disease manifestations and previous treatment experiences
- **Practice Setting + Resource Constraints**: Customizing messaging for providers in different practice environments with varying resource availability
- **Patient Population + Adherence Patterns**: Developing support resources for providers whose patients demonstrate specific adherence challenges

Benefits of Sophisticated Segmentation

- **Enhanced Relevance**: Healthcare providers receive information specifically aligned with their clinical practice realities
- **Improved Engagement**: More relevant messaging significantly increases content engagement and information retention
- **Optimized Resource Allocation**: Marketing resources focus on the audiences most likely to benefit from specific information

Ethical Considerations in Advanced Segmentation

As emphasized in Chapters 3 and 6, sophisticated segmentation requires careful ethical consideration:

- **Maintain Appropriate De-identification**: Ensure all segmentation uses properly anonymized data without re-identification risk
- **Focus on Educational Value**: Segmentation should enable delivery of genuinely valuable clinical information, not manipulation
- **Respect Provider Autonomy**: Recognize that segmentation informs educational approaches but should not attempt to unduly influence clinical decisions

8.2 Developing Targeted Communication Channels and Messaging Approaches

Aligning Channels with Audience Preferences and Information Needs

Building on the patient engagement principles discussed in Chapter 5 and the data-driven marketing strategies from Chapter 7, pharmaceutical companies must carefully select appropriate channels for different audience segments and communication objectives.

Audience-Centered Channel Selection

Effective communication begins with understanding how different healthcare audiences prefer to receive information:

- **Practice Setting Considerations**: Hospital-based specialists, community practitioners, and integrated delivery networks each have distinct information access patterns
- **Generational Preferences**: Significant variations exist in digital channel utilization across different provider age groups
- **Technological Adoption Patterns**: Health systems and practices demonstrate varied EHR integration levels and digital tool utilization

Channel Strategy Matrix

Audience Segment	Primary Channels	Secondary Channels	Content Emphasis
Academic Specialists	• Peer-reviewed publications • Medical congress presence • Digital scientific platforms	• Advisory board engagement • Speaker programs • Clinical trial opportunities	• Advanced scientific data • Mechanism of action • Research opportunities
Comm-unity Specialists	• EHR-integrated resources • Digital detailing • Professional society resources	• Peer-to-peer programs • Case-based education • Regional symposia	• Patient selection guidance • Practical implementation • Reimbursement support
Primary Care Providers	• EHR clinical decision support • Brief digital updates • Practice-focused education	• Patient education materials • Quick-reference guides • Diagnostic tools	• Screening /identification tools • Referral guidelines • Co-management approaches
Advanced Practice Providers	• Procedure-specific training • Patient management resources • Professional association channels	• Certification support • Patient education tools • Team-based care resources	• Practical implementation • Patient communication tools • Role-specific guidelines

FIGURE 8.4: Healthcare Provider Channel Strategy Matrix.

Message Development Principles

Once appropriate channels are identified, several principles guide effective message creation:

- **Clinical Value Prioritization**: Emphasize genuine clinical benefits and patient outcomes rather than product features
- **Evidence-Based Foundation**: Ground all communications in robust clinical evidence with appropriate context
- **Practical Implementation Focus**: Address real-world implementation considerations and challenges

Personalization Framework

Effective healthcare communication implements personalization across multiple dimensions:

- **Content Personalization**: Tailoring information depth, clinical focus, and supporting evidence to provider specialties and interests
- **Context Personalization**: Delivering information within relevant clinical workflow contexts and decision points
- **Format Personalization**: Adapting content format based on channel preferences and consumption patterns

Multichannel Integration Strategy

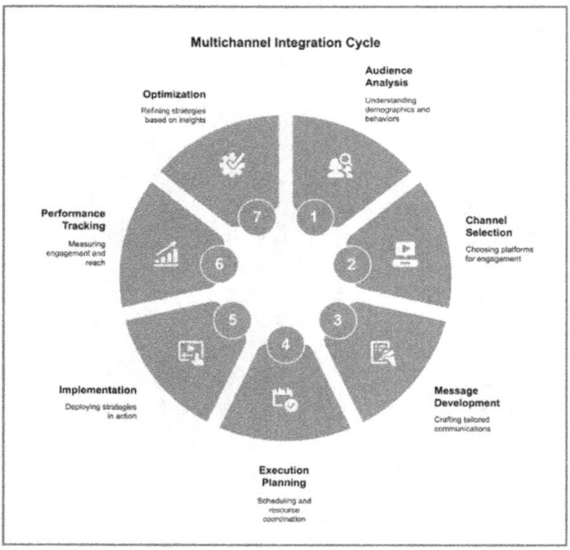

FIGURE 8.5: Integrated Multichannel Communication Cycle.

Content Transformation Across Channels

Effective multichannel strategies recognize that content must be appropriately adapted across different channels:

- **Channel-Appropriate Depth**: Scientific publications require comprehensive methodological details, while EHR alerts need concise, actionable information
- **Format Optimization**: Visual content works effectively in digital channels, while text-based content suits email communications
- **Interaction Capabilities**: Interactive tools enhance web platforms, while print materials benefit from scannable design elements

Measurement and Refinement

As discussed in section 8.3, continuous measurement enables ongoing refinement:

- **Channel-Specific Metrics**: Track engagement patterns across different communication platforms
- **Integrated Analytics**: Connect channel performance to overall communication objectives
- **Continuous Optimization**: Regularly refine channel mix based on performance data

8.3 Measuring the Effectiveness of EHR-Driven Marketing Campaigns

Data-Driven Assessment of Communication Impact

Building on the marketing measurement principles introduced in Chapter 7, pharmaceutical companies must implement comprehensive frameworks to evaluate EHR-driven communication effectiveness. This section outlines strategic approaches to campaign measurement that balance quantitative metrics with qualitative insights.

Comprehensive Measurement Framework

Before launching any EHR-informed campaign, establish a structured measurement approach with clearly defined metrics:

Engagement Metrics

- **Digital Interaction Rates**: Measure content consumption, including website visits, resource downloads, and video views
- **Email Engagement**: Track open rates, click-through patterns, and content interaction across email communications

- **EHR Integration Points**: Monitor utilization of EHR-embedded resources, clinical decision support tools, and information lookups

Conversion Metrics

- **Information Requests**: Measure provider-initiated requests for additional clinical information or resources
- **Prescribing Behavior**: Track changes in appropriate prescription patterns following educational initiatives
- **Patient Enrollment**: Monitor patient enrollment in support programs and educational resources

Brand Impact Metrics

- **Awareness Evolution**: Assess changes in product and indication awareness among target providers
- **Perception Shifts**: Measure changes in key perception attributes like efficacy understanding and safety perspectives
- **Educational Impact**: Evaluate improvements in disease state knowledge and appropriate patient identification

Integrated Measurement Dashboard

Metric Category	Leading Indicators	Lagging Indicators	Data Sources
Engagement	• Content interaction rates • Resource utilization • Digital tool adoption	• Sustained platform usage • Return visit frequency • Content sharing behavior	• Digital analytics • CRM data • Platform metrics
Clinical Impact	• Educational assessment scores • Clinical tool utilization • Information seeking behavior	• Prescribing pattern changes • Patient identification rates • Guideline adherence	• Claims data • Anonymized EHR data • Market research
Business Results	• Brand awareness metrics • Message recall rates • Competitive positioning	• Prescription volume • Market share evolution • New patient starts	• Prescription data • Market analytics • Financial reporting

FIGURE 8.6: Pharmaceutical Marketing Measurement Dashboard.

Advanced Measurement Approaches

A/B Testing Methodology

Implement structured testing to optimize communication effectiveness:

- **Message Variant Testing**: Compare different clinical message formulations to identify optimal approaches
- **Format Comparison**: Evaluate different content formats for information retention and engagement
- **Timing Optimization**: Test different message delivery timeframes to maximize impact

Attribution Modeling

Develop sophisticated models to understand how different touchpoints influence outcomes:

- **Multi-Touch Attribution**: Recognize that healthcare providers typically interact with multiple information sources before changing clinical behavior
- **Time-Decay Models**: Account for the different impact of interactions based on their timing relative to decision points
- **Channel Interaction Analysis**: Understand how different communication channels work together to influence outcomes

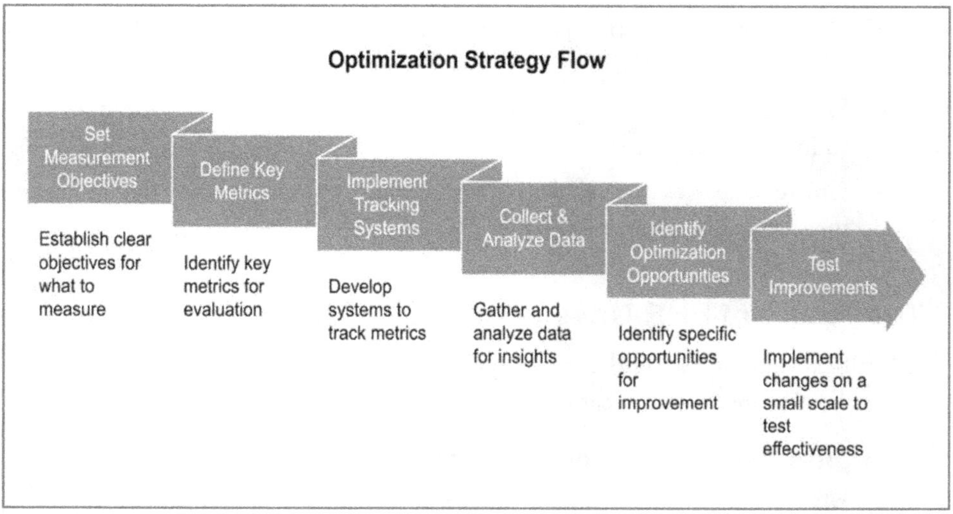

FIGURE 8.7: Continuous Measurement and Optimization Cycle.

Optimizing Messaging Strategies for Maximum Impact

Different healthcare stakeholders require tailored messaging approaches for optimal engagement:

For Healthcare Providers

- Ensure clinical decision support alerts are evidence-based and non-disruptive to workflow
- Prioritize contextually relevant information delivery at appropriate treatment decision points
- Leverage analytics to understand prescribing patterns and information needs

For Pharmaceutical Teams

- Use EHR-derived insights to develop content aligned with actual clinical challenges
- Ensure strict regulatory compliance by focusing on educational rather than promotional content
- Measure effectiveness through both engagement metrics and appropriate utilization outcomes

For Technology Developers & Data Scientists

- Design integration points that respect clinical workflows while providing valuable information
- Develop AI-enhanced messaging tools that learn from engagement patterns to improve relevance
- Create analytics frameworks that connect communication initiatives to meaningful outcomes

The Future of EHR-Driven Healthcare Messaging

As artificial intelligence and data analytics capabilities continue advancing, EHR-driven healthcare communication will evolve significantly:

Emerging Capabilities and Approaches

- **Predictive Engagement Systems**: AI systems that anticipate information needs based on clinical patterns and proactively deliver relevant content

- **Hyper-Personalized Education**: Machine learning algorithms that continuously optimize educational content based on individual learning patterns and preferences
- **Voice-Activated Clinical Intelligence**: Voice-enabled systems allowing providers to request specific information during patient encounters

Ethical Evolution

As these technologies advance, maintaining ethical principles becomes increasingly important:

- **Algorithmic Transparency**: Ensuring healthcare providers understand how AI systems select and deliver information
- **Balanced Implementation**: Developing systems that enhance rather than replace clinical judgment
- **Continuous Oversight**: Implementing governance frameworks that review messaging approaches for appropriate balance and accuracy

Final Thoughts: The Future of EHR-Driven Messaging

As technology continues to advance, EHR-driven communication will become increasingly sophisticated, transforming pharmaceutical engagement through:

- AI-powered systems providing real-time, contextually relevant clinical decision support
- Evidence-based, personalized education tailored to specific provider information needs
- Ethically designed communication approaches that enhance rather than interrupt patient care

Pharmaceutical companies and healthcare organizations that thoughtfully implement these advanced messaging approaches—while maintaining the ethical principles outlined throughout this book—will lead the evolution toward precision engagement that genuinely improves both provider decision-making and patient outcomes.

Chapter Nine

Building a Culture of Data-Driven Marketing in Pharma

Embracing Data as the Foundation for Market Access

The pharmaceutical industry is rapidly evolving from traditional marketing approaches toward sophisticated data-driven decision-making strategies. As explored throughout previous chapters, pharmaceutical organizations now have unprecedented opportunities to leverage EHR insights, real-world evidence (RWE), and AI-powered analytics to create more effective, targeted marketing initiatives. However, the transition to a fully data-driven marketing approach extends beyond implementing new technologies—it requires a fundamental cultural transformation embracing data literacy, rigorous compliance frameworks, and ethical engagement principles.

This chapter explores:

- How pharmaceutical companies can successfully foster an organization-wide data-driven culture
- Evidence-based case studies demonstrating successful cultural transformations
- Strategic approaches to overcoming key implementation challenges
- A comprehensive framework for implementing data-first strategies in pharmaceutical marketing

Why Data-Driven Marketing Matters in Pharmaceuticals

Building on the marketing principles discussed in Chapters 7 and 8, data-driven approaches deliver several strategic advantages:

- **Precision Targeting**: Reach the most appropriate healthcare professionals and patients with contextually relevant messaging based on specific clinical needs and practice patterns
- **Enhanced Campaign Performance**: Data-informed campaign development leads to measurably higher engagement rates and return on investment
- **Regulatory Compliance**: Structured data governance enables responsible and ethical data utilization while ensuring adherence to evolving industry regulations
- **Competitive Differentiation**: Organizations that effectively leverage healthcare insights gain significant advantages through more relevant engagement and stronger stakeholder relationships

Building the Organizational Foundation

Establishing a data-driven marketing culture requires systematic implementation of several foundational elements:

Executive Leadership Alignment

- Secure visible commitment from senior leadership to champion data-driven initiatives
- Establish clear communication about the strategic importance of data-driven approaches
- Allocate sufficient resources for technology, training, and implementation

Cross-Functional Collaboration

- Foster integrated teamwork between marketing, sales, medical affairs, and data science departments
- Create formalized processes for sharing insights across traditionally siloed functions
- Develop unified key performance indicators that align department objectives

Comprehensive Data Governance Framework

- Establish transparent policies for data collection, access, utilization, and security
- Implement privacy-by-design principles that proactively address regulatory requirements
- Create accountability mechanisms for ensuring ethical data practices

Data Capability Maturity Model for Pharmaceutical Organizations

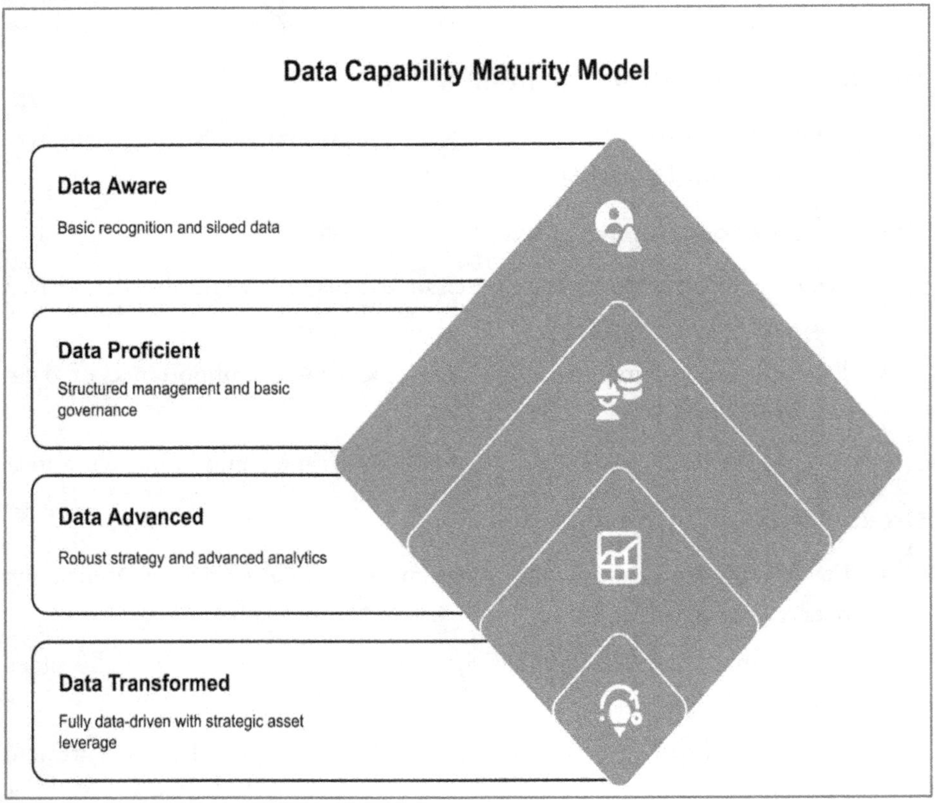

FIGURE 9.1: Data Capability Maturity Progression.

Maturity Level	Organizational Characteristics	Technology Requirements	People & Skills
Level 1: Data Aware	• Recognition of data's value • Initial data collection efforts • Minimal integration across systems	• Basic analytics tools • Limited automation • Fragmented data storage	• Limited data literacy • Few specialized data roles • Minimal training programs
Level 2: Data Proficient	• Structured data collection • Some cross-functional sharing • Established governance policies	• Integrated data platforms • Standardized analytics tools • Improved data security	• Growing data literacy • Dedicated data specialists • Regular training initiatives
Level 3: Data Advanced	• Data-informed decision processes • Cross-functional collaboration • Proactive compliance frameworks	• Advanced analytics capabilities • AI/ML implementation • Comprehensive data lakes	• Widespread data competency • Specialized analytics teams • Embedded data champions
Level 4: Data Transformed	• Data-driven culture embedded • Predictive decision-making • Innovation through insights	• AI-powered automation • Predictive modeling systems • Real-time analytics capabilities	• Organization-wide data fluency • Advanced data science expertise • Continuous learning environment

FIGURE 9.2: Pharmaceutical Data Maturity Model.

Investing in Data Infrastructure

To implement the data-driven approaches discussed in Chapters 7 and 8, pharmaceutical organizations must establish robust technological foundations:

Core Infrastructure Components

- **Data Management Platform (DMP)**: Centralized repository for collecting, storing, and managing healthcare provider and anonymized patient data
- **Customer Relationship Management (CRM) System**: Comprehensive tracking of healthcare provider interactions and engagement patterns
- **Marketing Automation Systems**: Tools for streamlining campaign development, audience segmentation, and personalized communication

Advanced Analytical Capabilities

- **Real-World Evidence Platforms**: Systems for analyzing de-identified patient data to derive actionable insights
- **Predictive Analytics Tools**: Solutions that model future behavior based on historical patterns
- **Natural Language Processing Systems**: Technologies that analyze unstructured medical data from clinical notes and scientific literature

Integration Architecture

- **API Frameworks**: Systems enabling secure data exchange between different platforms
- **Data Lakes**: Centralized repositories storing structured and unstructured data at scale
- **Visualization Tools**: Solutions that transform complex data into accessible, actionable insights

Developing Data-Driven Capabilities

Building on the marketing capabilities discussed in Chapter 7, pharmaceutical organizations must cultivate specialized skills:

Strategic Skill Development

- **Comprehensive Training Programs**: Develop structured learning paths for marketing teams covering data analysis, interpretation, and application
- **Data Science Expertise**: Build specialized in-house data science capabilities or establish strategic partnerships with analytics organizations
- **Data Literacy Initiatives**: Foster a culture where all team members understand data's value and role in driving marketing success

Data Capability Framework

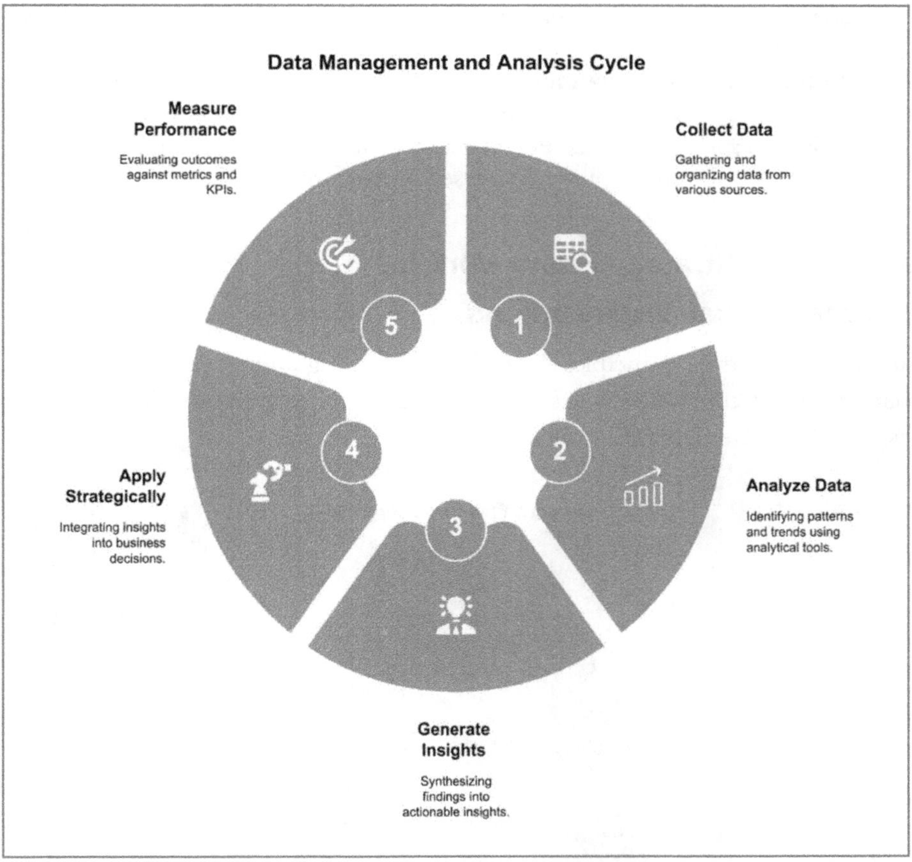

FIGURE 9.3: Data Capability Development Cycle.

Implementing Data-Driven Strategy in Pharmaceutical Marketing

As explored in Chapters 7 and 8, data-driven pharmaceutical marketing requires a structured implementation approach:

Strategic Implementation Process

1. **Define Success Metrics**: Establish clear key performance indicators aligned with specific marketing objectives
2. **Develop Segmentation Strategy**: Leverage data insights to create meaningful audience segments based on practice patterns, patient populations, and information needs
3. **Create Data-Informed Content**: Develop educational materials tailored to specific healthcare provider segments using real-world evidence and clinical insights
4. **Implement Omnichannel Engagement**: Deliver personalized messages through optimal channels based on engagement preferences
5. **Continuously Optimize Performance**: Monitor campaign results, analyze patterns, and refine approaches based on performance data

Data-Driven Strategy Framework for Pharmaceutical Organizations

Building on the principles established throughout previous chapters, pharmaceutical companies must establish a comprehensive strategic foundation based on four interdependent pillars:

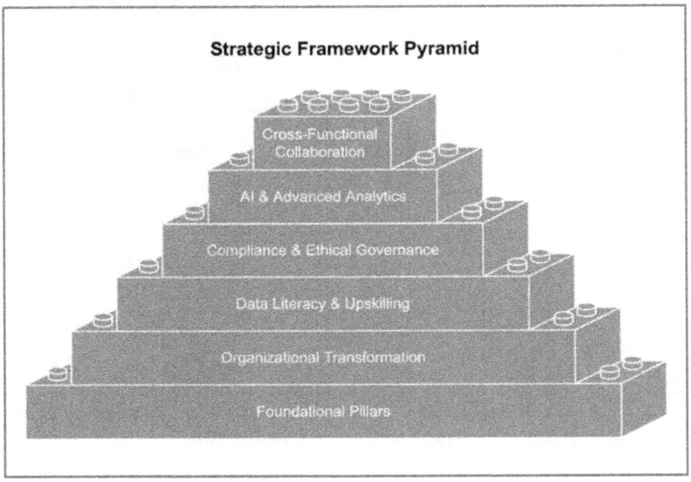

FIGURE 9.4: Data-Driven Pharmaceutical Strategy Framework.

1. **Data Literacy & Upskilling**
    - Ensure marketing teams develop the capabilities to effectively interpret and apply EHR insights
    - Implement ongoing education in AI-driven analytics and predictive modeling techniques
    - Develop specialized roles bridging marketing expertise with data science capabilities
2. **Compliance & Ethical Governance**
    - Establish comprehensive internal policies governing ethical use of healthcare data
    - Ensure rigorous adherence to regulations including HIPAA, GDPR, and emerging AI requirements
    - Implement proactive governance frameworks that anticipate regulatory developments
3. **AI & Advanced Analytics Integration**
    - Deploy machine learning models to predict engagement patterns and optimize messaging
    - Implement AI-powered personalization for targeted healthcare provider outreach
    - Develop natural language processing capabilities to derive insights from unstructured data
4. **Cross-Functional Collaboration**
    - Align marketing, data science, regulatory affairs, and IT teams to break down traditional silos
    - Establish unified objectives and shared metrics across departments
    - Create formalized knowledge-sharing processes to disseminate insights organization-wide

Case Study: Johnson & Johnson's Data Literacy Transformation

The Challenge: Data Literacy Gaps in Marketing Teams

Johnson & Johnson identified a significant capability gap limiting their ability to leverage data effectively. Despite substantial investments in data infrastructure, marketing teams lacked the skills to properly utilize EHR-derived insights. Traditional marketing approaches relied heavily on anecdotal sales representative feedback and broad demographic targeting, resulting in suboptimal healthcare provider engagement.

Contd...

Strategic Solution: Comprehensive Data Literacy Program

Johnson & Johnson implemented a structured six-month data literacy initiative encompassing:

- **Advanced Analytics Workshops**: Specialized training modules teaching marketers how to interpret complex prescribing patterns and identify meaningful engagement opportunities
- **Hands-On Applied Training**: Practical sessions utilizing anonymized EHR datasets to develop targeting strategies and message optimization
- **Cross-Functional Integration**: Structured collaboration between marketing teams and data science specialists to break down organizational silos

Measurable Outcomes

The initiative delivered significant business impact:

- 85% of marketing team members achieved proficiency in healthcare data analytics
- 30% improvement in campaign precision resulting in measurably higher engagement rates
- Enhanced regulatory compliance through more sophisticated data handling procedures

Key Implementation Insights

- Pharmaceutical marketing teams require specialized training in healthcare data analytics
- Hands-on practice with real-world datasets accelerates capability development
- Cross-functional collaboration ensures proper governance and more effective implementation

Source: Johnson & Johnson Digital Marketing Strategy Report (2022)

Overcoming Common Implementation Challenges

While data-driven marketing offers significant advantages, pharmaceutical organizations typically encounter several implementation obstacles:

1. **Organizational Resistance**

   Challenge: Many established pharmaceutical teams remain committed to traditional sales-driven approaches and resist adopting data-driven methodologies.

   Solution: Implement comprehensive change management strategies:

- Engage influential internal champions to demonstrate support
- Create pilot programs demonstrating tangible ROI improvements
- Develop clear communication about the strategic necessity of data transformation

2. **Data Interpretation Complexity**

   Challenge: Without proper training, marketing professionals may misinterpret healthcare data, leading to incorrect conclusions and ineffective campaigns.

   Solution: Implement structured data interpretation frameworks:

   - Develop standardized analytical approaches for common marketing scenarios
   - Create intuitive data visualization tools making insights accessible
   - Establish cross-functional review processes ensuring analytical quality

3. **Regulatory Navigation**

   Challenge: Pharmaceutical organizations must balance effective marketing with increasingly complex privacy regulations.

   Solution: Develop integrated compliance approaches:

   - Create proactive privacy-by-design frameworks embedding compliance into processes
   - Establish clear guidelines for appropriate healthcare data utilization
   - Implement regular compliance training and certification programs

4. **Organizational Silos**

   Challenge: Data insights often remain trapped within specific departments, preventing holistic understanding.

   Solution: Foster genuine cross-functional collaboration:

   - Implement integrated technology platforms enabling secure data sharing
   - Establish cross-functional teams with representation from key departments
   - Create shared objectives and metrics across traditionally separate functions

Implementation Challenge Matrix

Challenge Category	Common Manifestations	Strategic Solutions	Organizational Impact
Cultural Resistance	• "This isn't how we've always done it" • Skepticism about data accuracy • Preference for intuition-based decisions	• Pilot programs with measurable outcomes • Executive sponsorship of data initiatives • Recognition programs for data-driven success	• Accelerated adoption of data practices • Reduced resistance to new methodologies • Improved change readiness
Technical Complexity	• Overwhelming data volume • Difficulty connecting insights to actions • Inconsistent data quality	• Intuitive visualization dashboards • Guided analytical frameworks • Standardized data quality protocols	• More effective insight utilization • Improved confidence in data accuracy • Faster time-to-insight
Talent & Capability Gaps	• Limited analytical expertise • Insufficient data interpretation skills • Statistical concept misunderstanding	• Structured training programs • Data translation specialists • Simplified analytical tools	• Enhanced analytical capabilities • More accurate interpretation • Broader data utilization
Compliance Uncertainty	• Fear of regulatory violations • Overly restrictive data policies • Inconsistent governance practices	• Clear ethical guidelines • Embedded compliance checkpoints • Regular regulatory training	• Appropriate risk management • Compliant innovation • Consistent governance

FIGURE 9.5: Data Transformation Challenge Framework.

9.1 Fostering Collaboration Between Marketing, Medical Affairs and R&D Teams

Breaking Down Traditional Pharmaceutical Silos

Building on the cross-functional collaboration principles introduced in Chapter 7, pharmaceutical organizations must foster deeper integration between traditionally separate departments. Successful product development and commercialization depend on seamless collaboration between marketing, medical affairs, and R&D teams. While these departments possess distinct expertise, they share the common objective of bringing innovative therapies to appropriate patients.

Creating Collaborative Structures

- **Unified Vision Development**: Establish a clear, shared vision for product development and commercialization ensuring all departments understand strategic priorities
- **Integrated Project Teams**: Form dedicated cross-functional units with representation from marketing, medical affairs, and R&D for specific therapeutic initiatives
- **Formalized Knowledge Exchange**: Implement structured communication channels for sharing critical updates, discussing challenges, and developing collaborative solutions

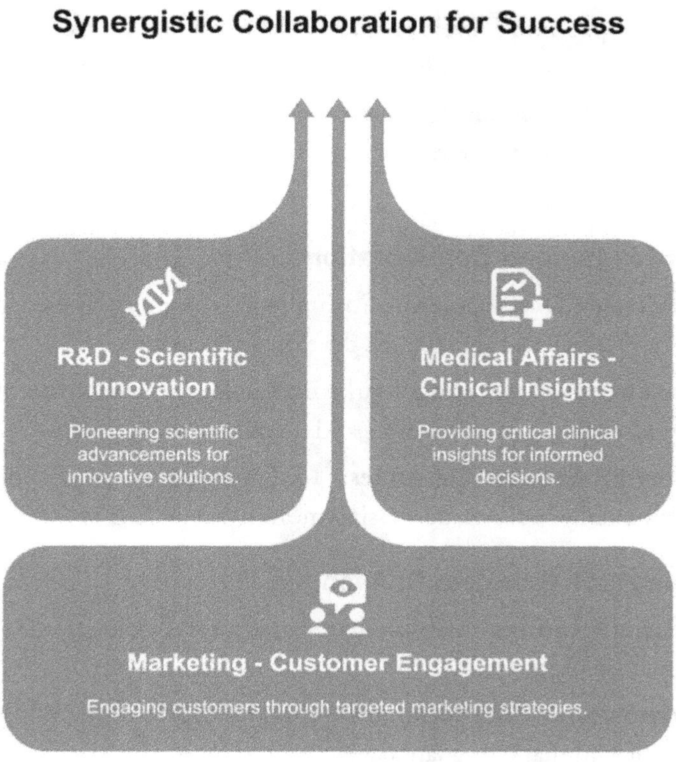

FIGURE 9.6: Integrated Pharmaceutical Expertise Model.

Each department contributes unique perspectives to the development and commercialization process:

- **R&D Contributions**: Deep scientific knowledge of product mechanisms, technical capabilities, and research methodologies
- **Medical Affairs Insights**: Comprehensive understanding of disease states, treatment landscapes, and unmet clinical needs
- **Marketing Expertise**: Sophisticated understanding of audience segmentation, messaging effectiveness, and engagement strategies

Collaborative Initiative Examples

- **Evidence Generation Planning**: Joint development of clinical trial designs and real-world evidence strategies addressing both scientific and commercial objectives
- **Value Proposition Development**: Collaborative creation of value narratives grounded in scientific evidence while addressing market needs
- **Educational Content Creation**: Integrated development of healthcare provider education leveraging scientific accuracy with engagement best practices

Benefits of Enhanced Collaboration

- **Accelerated Development**: Streamlined communication and aligned objectives accelerate therapeutic development timelines
- **More Effective Marketing**: Marketing teams gain access to deeper scientific insights, enabling more credible and impactful engagement
- **Improved Patient Outcomes**: Collaboration ensures all initiatives fundamentally focus on addressing meaningful patient needs

Overcoming Collaborative Challenges

- **Differing Priorities**: Establish shared metrics addressing both scientific and commercial objectives
- **Communication Barriers**: Create common terminology bridges between scientific and marketing language
- **Organizational Boundaries**: Implement matrix structures enabling flexible collaboration without disrupting departmental excellence

9.2 Investing in Data Literacy and Training for Marketing Professionals

Developing Critical Data Capabilities

As explored in Chapter 7, effective pharmaceutical marketing increasingly depends on sophisticated data utilization. Organizations must systematically develop these capabilities through strategic training and educational initiatives.

Data Literacy Benefits for Pharmaceutical Marketing

- **Enhanced Decision Quality**: Data-informed marketing decisions consistently outperform intuition-based approaches
- **Improved Targeting Precision**: Data-literate teams develop more sophisticated segmentation and targeting strategies
- **Optimized Resource Allocation**: Analytical capability enables more effective budget distribution across channels and initiatives
- **Strengthened Competitive Position**: Organizations with strong data capabilities consistently outperform less analytical competitors

Comprehensive Data Literacy Framework

Skill Category	Core Competencies	Application in Pharmaceutical Marketing
Foundational Data Understanding	• Basic statistical concepts • Data collection methodologies • Data quality assessment	• Interpreting research reports • Evaluating data validity • Understanding sampling limitations
Analytical Techniques	• Descriptive analytics • Trend identification • Correlation analysis	• Campaign performance analysis • Audience segmentation • Message optimization
Tool Proficiency	• Dashboard utilization • CRM data management • Marketing automation	• Performance tracking • Customer journey analysis • Campaign automation
Data Visualization	• Chart selection principles • Visual clarity techniques • Storytelling with data	• Executive presentations • Insight communication • Performance reporting
Ethical Data Usage	• Privacy principles • Regulatory requirements • Ethical frameworks	• Compliant targeting • Appropriate personalization • Responsible data collection

FIGURE 9.7: Pharmaceutical Marketing Data Literacy Framework.

Implementing Effective Data Training Programs

Training Program Components

- **Foundational Data Curriculum**: Courses covering basic statistical concepts, healthcare data structures, and analytical methodologies
- **Marketing Analytics Tools**: Hands-on training with relevant platforms including CRM systems, marketing automation tools, and analytics dashboards
- **Data Visualization Workshops**: Practical sessions on creating compelling visual representations of marketing insights
- **Data Storytelling Development**: Training on crafting compelling narratives based on data insights

Delivery Methodologies

- **Blended Learning Approaches**: Combine in-person workshops, virtual training, and self-paced modules
- **Role-Based Learning Paths**: Develop specialized curricula addressing specific role requirements
- **Continuous Education Programs**: Implement ongoing learning rather than one-time training events
- **Applied Learning Projects**: Integrate real business challenges into training for immediate application

Integrating Data Skills into Marketing Workflows

- **Data-Driven Planning Sessions**: Implement analytical approaches to campaign development and strategy
- **Insight-Generation Workshops**: Conduct structured analysis sessions extracting insights from marketing data
- **Experimentation Frameworks**: Develop A/B testing methodologies for continual message optimization
- **Data-Informed Performance Reviews**: Incorporate analytical assessment into regular performance evaluation

Measuring Training Effectiveness

- **Skill Assessment Evolution**: Evaluate capability development through pre/post-training assessments
- **Business Impact Analysis**: Measure improvements in marketing performance following training initiatives

- **Return on Training Investment**: Calculate financial benefits resulting from enhanced analytical capabilities

9.3 Building A Long-Term Vision Using EHRs to Improve Patient Care and Marketing Outcomes

Aligning Patient Benefits with Business Objectives

Building on the EHR applications discussed throughout previous chapters, pharmaceutical organizations must develop comprehensive long-term strategies integrating both patient care improvements and marketing effectiveness. This integrated approach creates sustainable value for all stakeholders.

Patient-Centered Care Enhancement

EHR systems provide numerous opportunities to improve patient outcomes:

- **Care Coordination Optimization**: Utilize EHR data to enhance communication and continuity across healthcare providers
- **Precision Medicine Advancement**: Leverage de-identified EHR data to identify specific patient populations benefiting from tailored interventions
- **Remote Monitoring Integration**: Connect EHR systems with monitoring technologies enabling proactive care management

Example: A pharmaceutical company partners with healthcare systems to implement an EHR-integrated program identifying patients with specific genetic markers who would benefit from a targeted therapy, improving treatment selection while supporting appropriate medication utilization.

Data-Informed Engagement Strategy

Building on the messaging approaches outlined in Chapter 8, EHR insights enable more sophisticated engagement:

- **Precision Audience Segmentation**: Analyze de-identified clinical and demographic patterns to develop highly relevant audience segments
- **Patient Education Enhancement**: Develop EHR-integrated resources providing personalized health information and treatment support
- **Relationship Strengthening**: Foster deeper provider and patient connections through more relevant, valuable interactions

Example: A pharmaceutical manufacturer creates disease management resources for specific patient segments identified through anonymized EHR analysis, delivering these materials through healthcare provider channels to improve both clinical outcomes and brand perception.

Innovation Through Data Integration

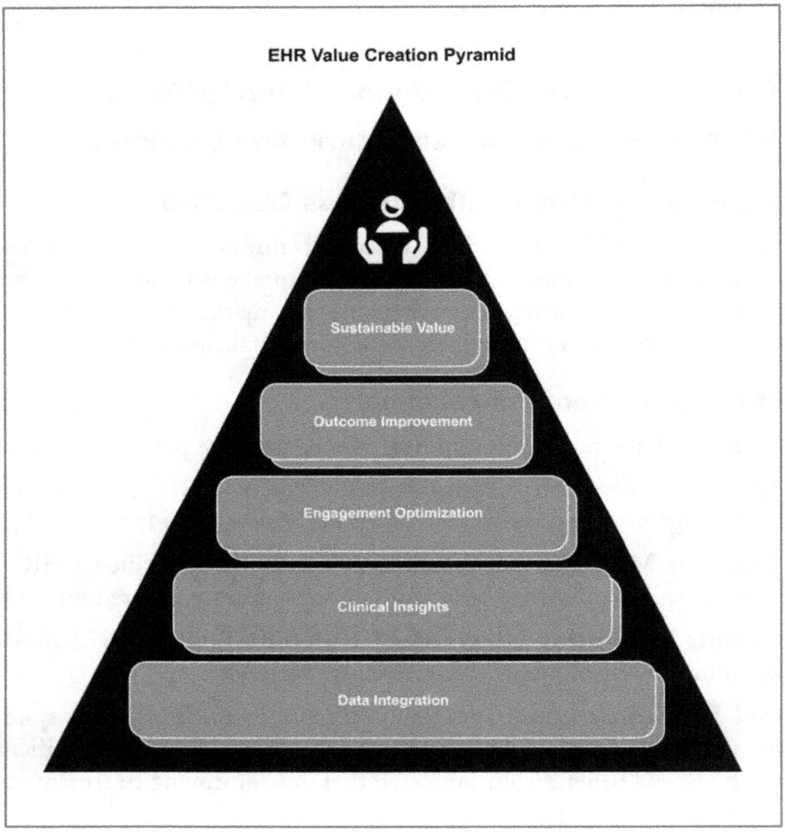

FIGURE 9.8: Integrated EHR Value Creation Model.

Forward-looking pharmaceutical organizations implement several strategic initiatives:

- **Advanced Analytics Infrastructure**: Develop sophisticated capabilities to derive meaningful insights from complex healthcare data
- **Strategic Technology Partnerships**: Collaborate with innovative technology companies creating novel EHR-integrated solutions
- **Data-Driven Culture Development**: Foster organizational mindsets prioritizing evidence-based decision-making

Example: A pharmaceutical company partners with a healthcare AI firm to develop a machine learning algorithm identifying patients at risk for medication non-adherence, enabling proactive intervention through healthcare provider channels while improving treatment effectiveness.

Case Study: Pfizer's AI-Powered EHR Analytics for Precision Marketing

The Challenge: Suboptimal Market Positioning

Pfizer encountered significant difficulties efficiently targeting physicians for a new cardiovascular therapy, resulting in lower-than-expected initial adoption rates despite the treatment's clinical benefits. Traditional targeting approaches based on specialty designation and prescription volume failed to identify the most appropriate providers effectively.

Strategic Solution: AI-Enhanced EHR Analytics Implementation

Pfizer implemented a sophisticated AI-powered predictive analytics approach:

- **Advanced Prescribing Pattern Analysis**: Utilized anonymized EHR data to identify healthcare providers managing patients most likely to benefit from the therapy
- **Behavioral Segmentation**: Categorized physicians based on observed treatment approaches and patient population characteristics
- **Content Optimization**: Tailored educational materials and engagement strategies to align with specific practice patterns

Measurable Outcomes

The initiative delivered substantial performance improvements:

- 25% increase in appropriate prescriptions within specifically targeted physician segments
- Significant marketing efficiency improvements through more precise resource allocation
- Enhanced healthcare provider relationships through more relevant, valuable engagement

Key Implementation Insights

- AI-enhanced predictive analytics significantly improves the effectiveness of EHR-based marketing
- Segmentation based on actual treatment patterns enables more precise targeting than traditional methods
- Data-driven approaches can simultaneously improve engagement effectiveness while enhancing compliance

Source: Pfizer AI & EHR Analytics Report (2022)

Actionable Insights: Implementing a Data-First Marketing Strategy

For Pharmaceutical Organizations

- Invest in comprehensive data literacy development across marketing functions
- Leverage advanced analytics to continuously refine targeting approaches and messaging
- Integrate robust compliance frameworks throughout all data-driven marketing processes
- Foster genuine collaboration between marketing, data science, and compliance teams

For Healthcare Providers

- Engage with data-informed resources improving treatment decision quality
- Collaborate with pharmaceutical partners on evidence-based adherence improvement
- Utilize AI-enhanced clinical decision support tools providing real-world treatment insights

For Data Science & Analytics Teams

- Develop sophisticated marketing optimization tools with embedded compliance safeguards
- Create intuitive data visualization dashboards making insights accessible to non-technical users
- Refine predictive models enhancing the accuracy of prescribing behavior forecasts

For Compliance & Legal Teams

- Design privacy-by-design frameworks enabling compliant data utilization
- Develop clear guidelines for appropriate anonymized data application
- Implement proactive review processes ensuring regulatory adherence while enabling innovation

Ethical Framework for Data-Driven Pharmaceutical Marketing

Ethical Principle	Implementation Approach	Measurement Criteria
Patient Privacy Protection	• Comprehensive de-identification protocols • Minimal necessary data utilization • Purpose limitation frameworks	• De-identification audit results • Privacy impact assessments • Regulatory compliance verification
Transparency & Honesty	• Clear data usage disclosure • Explicit consent procedures • Accessible privacy policies	• Consent documentation • Privacy policy clarity assessment • Transparency reporting
Patient Benefit Prioritization	• Outcome improvement focus • Genuine educational content • Appropriate targeting principles	• Patient outcome measures • Educational value assessment • Targeting criteria review
Healthcare Provider Respect	• Non-disruptive workflow integration • Valuable information provision • Professional autonomy preservation	• Provider satisfaction metrics • Content utility measurement • Engagement quality assessment
Equitable Access Promotion	• Diverse population inclusion • Healthcare disparity consideration • Accessibility accommodation	• Demographic representation analysis • Access barrier assessment • Inclusion measurement

FIGURE 9.9: Ethical Framework for Data-Driven Pharmaceutical Marketing.

Final Thoughts: The Future of Data-Driven Pharmaceutical Marketing

As artificial intelligence and machine learning capabilities continue evolving, pharmaceutical marketing approaches will become increasingly sophisticated and effective:

Emerging Capabilities

- **Automated Insight Generation**: AI systems automatically extracting actionable insights from complex healthcare data
- **Predictive Engagement Optimization**: Machine learning algorithms continuously improving targeting and messaging effectiveness
- **Real-World Evidence Integration**: Seamless incorporation of treatment outcomes data into marketing strategy development

Future Success Factors

- **Data Ethics Leadership**: Organizations establishing industry-leading ethical standards for data utilization
- **Integrated Technology Ecosystems**: Seamless connection between diverse data sources and marketing execution systems
- **Continuous Capability Development**: Ongoing evolution of analytical skills and data literacy across marketing functions

By embracing data as a core strategic pillar while maintaining unwavering commitment to ethical principles, pharmaceutical companies will develop more effective, efficient, and responsible engagement strategies—ultimately benefiting healthcare providers, patients, and the broader healthcare ecosystem.

PART THREE: THE FUTURE OF EHRs AND HEALTHCARE INNOVATION

Part Three

The Future of EHRs and Healthcare Innovation

As we look toward the horizon of healthcare's digital transformation, the convergence of emerging technologies with Electronic Health Records promises to fundamentally reshape how care is delivered, how treatments are developed, and how patients engage with their health journey. Having explored the foundations of EHR systems and their strategic applications in pharmaceutical marketing, we now turn our attention to the future—examining both the transformative potential and critical considerations that will define healthcare's next chapter.

The final section of this book ventures beyond current capabilities to explore how artificial intelligence, blockchain, advanced analytics, and other emerging technologies will transform EHRs from passive documentation systems into dynamic, intelligent platforms that actively contribute to clinical decision-making and patient care. We will examine the ethical frameworks required to guide this evolution, ensuring that technological advancement enhances rather than diminishes the human dimensions of healthcare.

In Chapter 10, we explore the cutting-edge technologies poised to revolutionize EHR functionality, from AI-powered predictive analytics to blockchain security solutions and wearable integration. We examine not just theoretical possibilities but practical implementations and emerging best practices that are already demonstrating value in real-world environments.

Chapter 11 delves into the complex ethical considerations that must guide healthcare's digital future. As EHR systems become more powerful and autonomous, establishing robust frameworks for privacy, equity, transparency, and appropriate human oversight becomes increasingly essential. We explore how to balance innovation with responsibility, ensuring that technological advancement serves rather than subverts our most fundamental healthcare values.

Our journey concludes with Chapter 12, which synthesizes the technological, strategic, and ethical dimensions explored throughout the book into a comprehensive vision of healthcare's digital future. We provide actionable guidance for healthcare organizations and pharmaceutical companies preparing to navigate this rapidly evolving landscape, with strategic frameworks for implementation and governance.

Throughout Part 3, we maintain our focus on both the extraordinary potential of these technologies and the responsibility that comes with their implementation. The future of healthcare will be shaped not merely by what technology can do, but by how we choose to apply it in service of better patient outcomes, more efficient care delivery, and more equitable health systems.

As we explore these emerging frontiers, we invite readers to envision a healthcare ecosystem where technology enhances human capabilities rather than replacing them—where EHRs serve as intelligent partners to clinicians and empowering tools for patients. This vision of technology-enabled, human-centered healthcare provides the foundation for the innovations, strategies, and ethical frameworks explored in the chapters ahead.

Chapter Ten

Emerging Technologies in EHRs – The Future of Patient-Centric Care

Introduction: The Next Frontier in EHR Evolution

Over the past two decades, Electronic Health Records have evolved dramatically from the basic digital repositories described in Chapter 1 to sophisticated platforms enabling data-driven decision-making, predictive analytics, and real-time patient engagement as explored in Chapters 5 through 9. However, the next decade promises even more transformative advancements. The future of EHRs will be shaped by artificial intelligence, blockchain security, interoperability breakthroughs, and increasingly patient-centered innovations.

This chapter explores:

- How AI, blockchain, and enhanced interoperability are fundamentally reshaping EHR capabilities
- A detailed case study on blockchain security implementation with MIT's groundbreaking MedRec project
- Future-focused analysis of EHR evolution through 2030 and beyond
- A balanced examination of AI's benefits and potential risks in healthcare delivery

The Evolving Landscape of EHR Technology

Building on the foundational understanding of EHR systems established in previous chapters, we now look toward emerging technologies poised to transform healthcare information management. While Chapters 1 and 2 examined current EHR capabilities, the technologies discussed here represent the next generation of healthcare information systems.

Enhanced Interoperability and Seamless Data Exchange

As discussed in Chapter 2, limitations in data exchange between disparate EHR systems continue to restrict the flow of critical patient information. The future points toward comprehensive interoperability solutions:

- **Advanced API Frameworks**: Standardized application programming interfaces will enable secure, efficient communication between previously siloed EHR platforms
- **FHIR Standard Implementation**: The Fast Healthcare Interoperability Resources standard represents a significant advancement in healthcare data exchange, creating a common language for system interoperability
- **Universal Patient Identifiers**: Emerging systems for securely identifying patients across different healthcare organizations will resolve current matching challenges

Impact: True interoperability will foster holistic views of patient health, dramatically improve care coordination, and empower patients with unprecedented control over their health information.

Artificial Intelligence Integration

Building on the data analytics approaches discussed in Chapter 7, artificial intelligence will transform how healthcare organizations derive value from EHR data:

- **Advanced Predictive Analytics**: AI algorithms will analyze comprehensive patient datasets to predict health risks with unprecedented accuracy, enabling earlier interventions
- **Sophisticated Clinical Decision Support**: AI-powered systems will provide real-time treatment recommendations based on patient-specific data and continuously updated medical evidence
- **Natural Language Processing**: Advanced NLP capabilities will transform unstructured clinical notes into structured, actionable data while reducing documentation burden

Impact: AI integration will significantly enhance diagnostic accuracy, enable truly personalized treatment planning, and optimize healthcare resource allocation across populations.

Blockchain Technology for Enhanced Data Security

Expanding on the security frameworks outlined in Chapter 3, blockchain technology offers revolutionary approaches to health data protection:

- **Distributed Ledger Architecture**: Blockchain's decentralized structure ensures tamper-proof storage of sensitive patient information
- **Smart Contract Implementation**: Automated consent management through blockchain smart contracts gives patients granular control over data access
- **Immutable Audit Trails**: Blockchain creates permanent, unalterable records of all data access and modifications

Impact: Blockchain implementation will fundamentally transform patient data ownership, dramatically enhance security protections, and create unprecedented transparency in health information management.

EHR Evolution Maturity Model

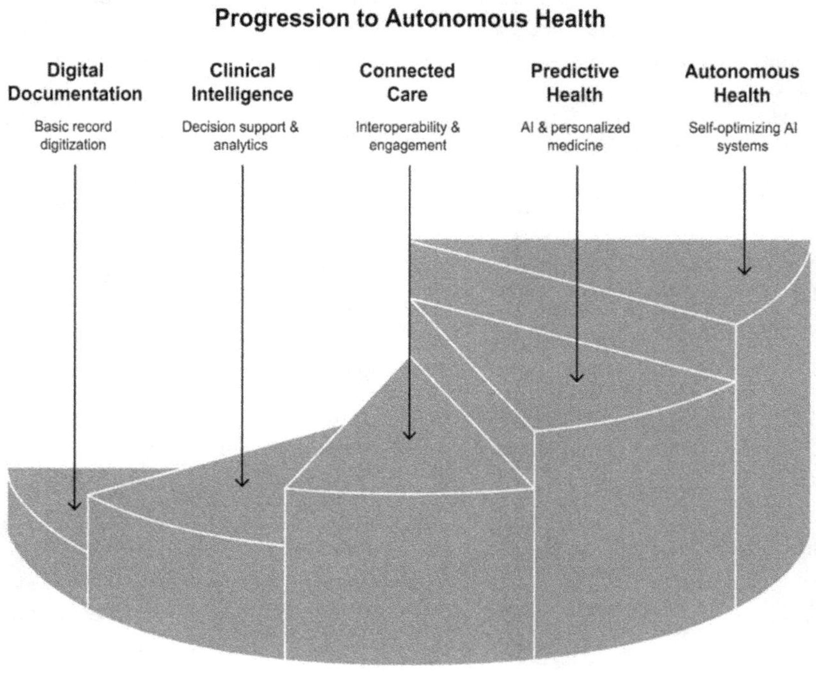

FIGURE 10.1: EHR Technology Evolution Maturity Model.

Evolution Phase	Core Technologies	Primary Value	Healthcare Impact
Digital Documentation (2000-2010)	• Basic EMR systems • Document scanning • Structured data entry	• Paper reduction • Improved legibility • Basic searchability	• Reduced clerical errors • Enhanced record accessibility • Foundation for further advancement
Clinical Intelligence (2010-2020)	• Clinical decision support • Basic analytics • Quality reporting tools	• Evidence-based alerts • Population reporting • Regulatory compliance	• Improved guideline adherence • Quality metric improvement • Enhanced safety protocols
Connected Care (2020-2025)	• Interoperability standards • Patient portals • Care coordination tools	• Information exchange • Patient engagement • Team-based care	• Reduced care fragmentation • Improved patient experience • Enhanced care continuity
Predictive Health (2025-2030)	• AI/ML integration • Blockchain security • Precision medicine tools	• Personalized risk prediction • Tailored interventions • Patient-owned data	• Earlier disease detection • More precise treatments • Preventive care optimization
Autonomous Health (2030+)	• Self-optimizing AI • Ambient clinical intelligence • Virtual care assistants	• Automatic documentation • Continuous learning systems • Frictionless workflows	• Provider focus on human aspects of care • Algorithmic treatment optimization • Unprecedented clinical efficiency

FIGURE 10.2: EHR Evolution Timeline and Impact Analysis.

Integration with Patient-Generated Health Data

Building on the patient engagement strategies discussed in Chapter 5, next-generation EHRs will seamlessly incorporate data from numerous patient-controlled sources:

- **Wearable Devices**: Continuous monitoring through smartwatches, fitness trackers, and specialized medical wearables
- **Remote Monitoring Systems**: Home-based devices tracking vital signs, medication adherence, and disease-specific parameters
- **Patient-Reported Outcomes**: Structured data collection directly from patients about symptoms, functioning, and quality of life

Impact: This integration will create unprecedented continuous health monitoring, enabling more personalized care planning and proactive intervention before conditions deteriorate.

Enhanced Patient Engagement and Usability

As explored in Chapter 5, EHR evolution increasingly emphasizes patient-centered design and functionality:

- **Intuitive Patient Interfaces**: User-friendly mobile applications and web portals allowing patients to easily navigate complex health information
- **Personalized Health Management Tools**: AI-powered applications providing customized recommendations based on individual health profiles
- **Bidirectional Communication Platforms**: Seamless engagement between patients and providers through secure messaging, telehealth, and automated check-ins

Impact: These advancements will foster greater patient ownership of health data, promote active participation in care decisions, and strengthen provider-patient relationships.

10.1 The Rise of Artificial Intelligence and Machine Learning in EHR Data Analysis Unveiling Hidden Patterns in Healthcare Data

Electronic Health Records contain extraordinary volumes of clinical data, as detailed in Chapter 2. However, manually analyzing this information is increasingly impractical given its complexity and scale. Artificial intelligence and machine learning technologies are revolutionizing EHR data analysis, uncovering previously hidden patterns and generating actionable insights that transform healthcare delivery.

Understanding the AI/ML Foundation

- **Machine Learning**: Algorithmic systems that learn from large datasets to identify patterns and make predictions without explicit programming
- **Artificial Intelligence**: The broader field encompassing ML, natural language processing, computer vision, and other technologies enabling machines to simulate human cognitive functions

Transforming EHR Data Analysis Through AI/ML Applications

Building on the data analytics approaches discussed in Chapter 7, AI and ML enable several advanced capabilities:

Disease Prediction and Risk Stratification

AI algorithms analyze comprehensive patient histories, laboratory results, and medication data to predict disease development risk with remarkable accuracy. This enables:

- Identification of pre-diabetic patients years before clinical manifestation
- Early detection of cardiovascular disease risk based on subtle pattern recognition
- Prediction of hospital readmission risk to enable targeted interventions

Example: A healthcare system implements an AI model that analyzes EHR data to identify patients at highest risk for sepsis up to 24 hours before clinical signs appear, enabling earlier intervention and significantly reducing mortality.

Advanced Clinical Decision Support

AI-powered systems analyze real-time patient data alongside vast medical knowledge bases to provide sophisticated decision support at the point of care:

- Medication dosing recommendations based on patient-specific factors
- Diagnostic assistance through pattern recognition in complex cases
- Treatment optimization based on similar patient outcomes analysis

Example: An AI clinical decision support system analyzes thousands of similar cases to recommend the optimal antibiotic regimen for a patient with complicated pneumonia, considering local resistance patterns, patient-specific factors, and latest evidence.

Precision Medicine Advancement

ML models analyze patient genetic information alongside clinical data to enable truly personalized treatment approaches:

- Prediction of medication response based on genetic variants
- Identification of optimal therapy selection for specific cancer subtypes
- Personalized disease management strategies based on comprehensive patient profiles

Example: An oncology AI platform analyzes tumor genetic profiles and treatment outcomes from thousands of similar cases to recommend the optimal chemotherapy protocol for an individual patient, significantly improving response rates.

AI/ML Implementation Architecture for Healthcare

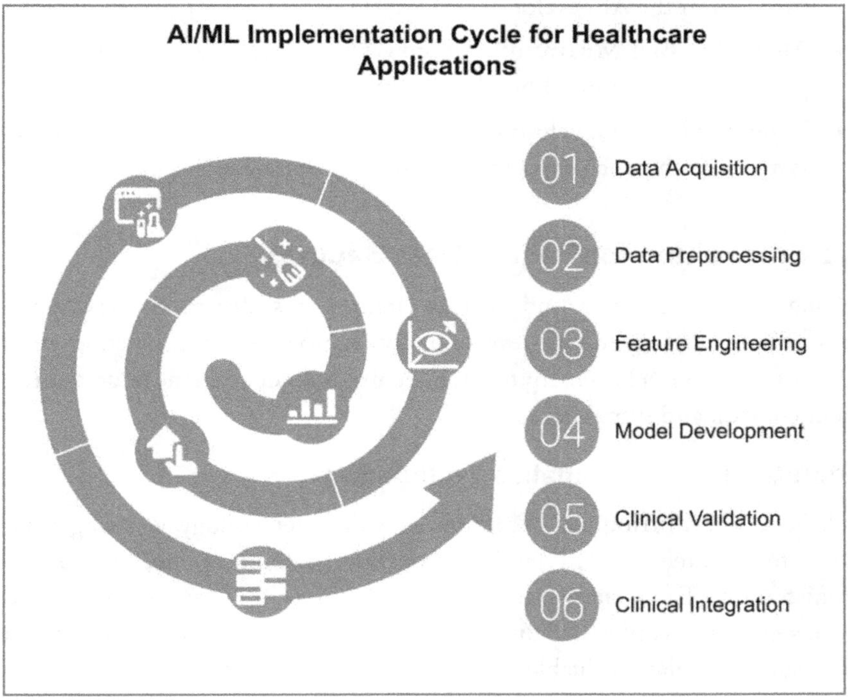

FIGURE 10.3: AI/ML Implementation Cycle for Healthcare Applications.

Benefits of AI/ML Integration in EHR Systems

- **Enhanced Diagnostic Accuracy**: AI systems can identify subtle patterns humans might miss, improving diagnostic precision
- **Operational Efficiency**: Automation of routine cognitive tasks frees clinical time for direct patient care
- **Population Health Management**: Advanced analytics enable more effective resource allocation and preventive interventions
- **Research Acceleration**: Machine learning can identify novel treatment patterns and research hypotheses from real-world data

Addressing AI Implementation Challenges

Several critical challenges must be addressed for responsible AI deployment:

- **Data Quality and Standardization**: AI performance depends on high-quality, standardized training data
- **Privacy and Security**: Robust safeguards must protect patient data throughout the AI development lifecycle
- **Algorithm Bias Mitigation**: Rigorous testing and diverse training data help prevent perpetuation of healthcare disparities
- **Explainable AI Development**: Clinicians need transparency into how AI systems reach conclusions to maintain appropriate oversight

10.2 Blockchain for Patient Data Security

Building on the security and privacy frameworks discussed in Chapter 3, blockchain technology offers revolutionary approaches to protecting sensitive health information. This emerging architecture provides enhanced data integrity, patient control, and system security.

Understanding Blockchain's Foundation

Blockchain is a distributed, decentralized ledger technology allowing multiple parties to securely record and share data without requiring centralized administration. Each transaction is cryptographically secured and linked to previous entries, creating an immutable chain of blocks. This architecture makes blockchain particularly valuable for healthcare data security.

Key Blockchain Features for Healthcare Security

Decentralized Architecture

Unlike traditional databases controlled by single entities, blockchain operates across distributed peer-to-peer networks, providing:

- Elimination of single failure points that could compromise entire systems
- Reduced vulnerability to centralized attacks or breaches
- Enhanced system reliability through distributed validation

Immutable Record Integrity

Once data is recorded on a properly implemented blockchain, it cannot be altered without network consensus:

- Tamper-evident design ensures any unauthorized modification attempts are immediately detectable
- Comprehensive audit trail records all data access and modifications
- Permanent, unalterable medical record history maintains clinical documentation integrity

Transparent Yet Private Data Management

Blockchain enables unprecedented transparency while maintaining appropriate privacy:

- Real-time tracking of all data access and modifications
- Granular permission controls enable selective information sharing
- Cryptographic techniques protect sensitive information while allowing verified transactions

Enhanced Security Implementation

Advanced cryptographic methods provide robust protection for healthcare data:

- Public and private key infrastructure ensures only authorized access
- Cryptographic validation prevents unauthorized data manipulation
- Secure multi-party computation enables analysis without exposing underlying data

Blockchain Implementation for Healthcare Data

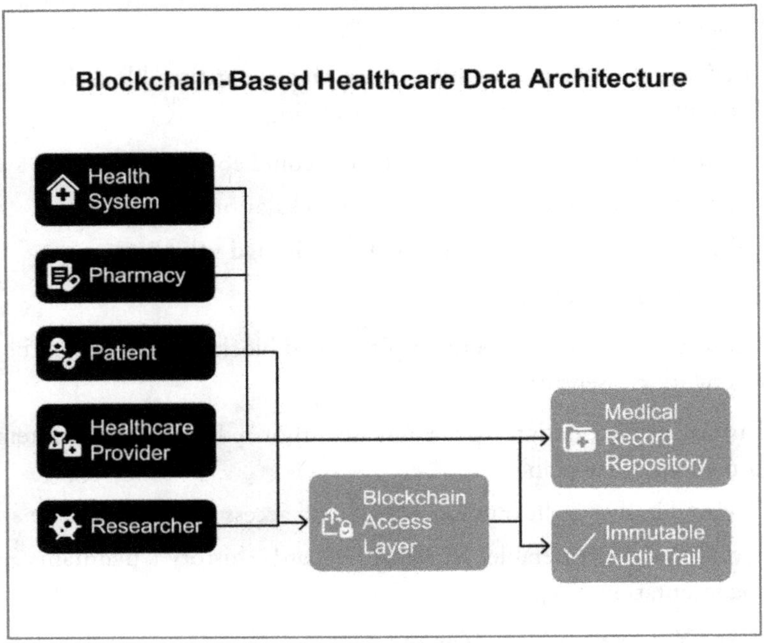

FIGURE 10.4: Blockchain-Based Healthcare Data Architecture.

Healthcare Applications of Blockchain Technology

Application Area	Implementation Approach	Security Benefits	Patient Benefits
Medical Records	Patient-controlled access keys Distributed storage with encryption Smart contract-based permissions	Tamper-proof history Breach risk reduction Comprehensive audit trails	Complete record ownership Granular access control Lifetime record portability
Medication Management	Pharmaceutical supply chain tracking Prescription verification Adherence monitoring	Counterfeit prevention Prescription fraud reduction Medication history integrity	Medication authenticity verification Complete medication history Safer prescription management

Contd...

Application Area	Implementation Approach	Security Benefits	Patient Benefits
Clinical Trials	Consent management Protocol adherence verification Outcome recording	Data tampering prevention Protocol violation detection Reliable outcome verification	Enhanced consent transparency Greater trial confidence Simplified participation management
Insurance Claims	Automated claim verification Smart contract-based processing Coverage transparency	Fraud reduction Process manipulation prevention Payment verification	Faster claim processing Greater billing transparency Reduced payment disputes

FIGURE 10.5: Blockchain Applications in Healthcare Security.

Case Study: MIT's MedRec Project

The Challenge: Patient Control Over Medical Data

Traditional EHR systems provide patients limited visibility and control over their own health records. Data sharing between providers remains fragmented and vulnerable to breaches, unauthorized access, and inefficiencies in care coordination.

Strategic Solution: Blockchain-Based Record Management

MIT researchers developed MedRec, an innovative blockchain-based EHR system that:

- Stores access metadata in a tamper-proof distributed ledger, ensuring security and transparency
- Enables patients to grant or revoke provider access through cryptographic private keys
- Creates comprehensive auditable data trails tracking every instance of record access
- Maintains actual health data in traditional databases while using blockchain for access control

Measurable Outcomes

The MedRec implementation demonstrated several significant advantages:

- Patients gained unprecedented control over who could access their records

Contd...

- Tamper-proof logging enhanced compliance with regulations including HIPAA and GDPR
- The architecture established potential pathways toward global EHR standardization
- The system significantly reduced cross-border health information exchange challenges

Key Implementation Insights

- Blockchain architecture effectively decentralizes patient data control, shifting authority to individuals
- Smart contracts provide automated enforcement of access policies, improving security and compliance
- Next-generation EHR systems will increasingly incorporate blockchain elements to enhance data integrity and privacy

Source: MIT MedRec Blockchain Research (2022)

Implementation Challenges and Considerations

Despite blockchain's considerable potential, several challenges must be addressed:

- **Regulatory Compliance**: Healthcare organizations must navigate complex privacy regulations when implementing blockchain solutions
- **Scalability Concerns**: Current blockchain implementations may struggle with the immense volume of healthcare data
- **Legacy System Integration**: Connecting blockchain solutions with existing healthcare IT infrastructure requires careful planning
- **Technical Expertise Development**: Organizations must develop specialized blockchain knowledge within their teams

10.3 The Integration of Wearables and Other Health Data Sources with EHR Systems

Building on the patient engagement strategies discussed in Chapter 5, next-generation EHR systems are increasingly incorporating data from wearable devices and other external health monitoring tools. This integration creates a more comprehensive view of patient health beyond traditional clinical encounters.

Creating a Continuous Health Monitoring Ecosystem

Traditional EHRs primarily capture episodic snapshots of patient health during clinical visits. The integration of wearables and other monitoring technologies enables:

- **Continuous Physiological Monitoring**: Real-time tracking of vital signs, activity levels, and sleep patterns
- **Contextual Health Understanding**: Documentation of health parameters within patients' daily environments
- **Early Warning Detection**: Identification of subtle changes preceding clinical deterioration
- **Behavioral Pattern Recognition**: Insights into lifestyle factors affecting health outcomes

Wearable Technology Integration Framework

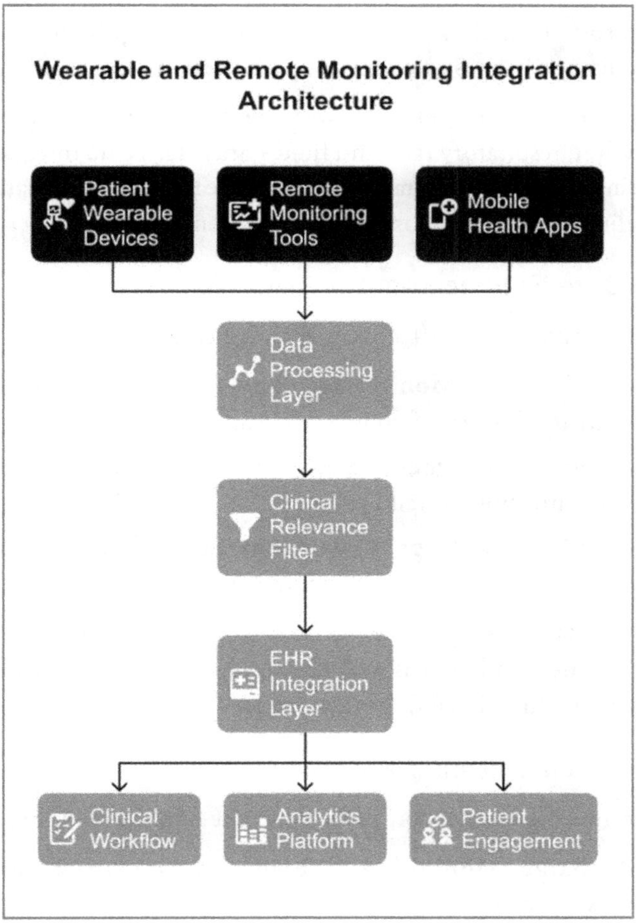

FIGURE 10.6: Wearable and Remote Monitoring Integration Architecture.

Strategic Applications of Integrated Health Data

Chronic Disease Management

Continuous monitoring transforms management of conditions like diabetes, heart failure, and COPD:

- **Real-Time Glucose Monitoring**: Continuous glucose monitors transmit blood sugar readings directly to EHR systems, enabling timely intervention and medication adjustments
- **Cardiac Parameter Tracking**: Wearable ECG devices detect arrhythmias and other cardiac abnormalities between office visits
- **Respiratory Function Assessment**: Connected spirometry devices track lung function changes, allowing early intervention for COPD exacerbations

Example: A heart failure patient uses a wearable patch that continuously monitors heart rate, rhythm, respiratory rate, and fluid status. This data integrates with their EHR, triggering alerts when parameters suggest early decompensation, enabling medication adjustment before hospitalization becomes necessary.

Preventive Care Enhancement

Wearable data supports more effective preventive care strategies:

- **Physical Activity Monitoring**: Fitness trackers provide objective measurement of exercise frequency and intensity
- **Sleep Quality Assessment**: Sleep tracking devices detect patterns and disruptions affecting overall health
- **Stress Level Monitoring**: Wearables measuring heart rate variability and other markers help quantify stress impacts

Example: A primary care practice analyzes activity tracker data from patient populations to identify individuals with decreasing activity levels, enabling targeted interventions before functional decline progresses.

Remote Patient Monitoring Programs

Integrated monitoring enables comprehensive care outside traditional settings:

- **Post-Discharge Monitoring**: Wearable devices track vital signs and symptoms following hospital discharge
- **Medication Adherence Tracking**: Smart pill dispensers and ingestible sensors document medication compliance

- **Rehabilitation Progress Measurement**: Connected devices track recovery metrics during home-based rehabilitation

Example: An elderly patient recovering from pneumonia returns home with a multiparameter monitoring patch. The data flows directly to their EHR, allowing the care team to monitor respiratory rate, oxygen levels, and temperature remotely, intervening promptly if recovery deviates from expected patterns.

Implementation Considerations for Connected Health

Several critical factors influence successful integration of wearable data:

Data Quality and Validation

- **Device Accuracy Assessment**: Evaluation of measurement precision across different wearable technologies
- **Contextual Understanding**: Algorithms accounting for situational factors affecting physiological measurements
- **Signal-to-Noise Filtering**: Processes distinguishing clinically meaningful signals from background variation

Clinical Workflow Integration

- **Alert Threshold Optimization**: Carefully calibrated notification systems preventing alarm fatigue
- **Data Visualization Design**: Intuitive interfaces presenting wearable data alongside traditional clinical information
- **Care Team Responsibility Delineation**: Clear protocols for responding to wearable-generated alerts

Technical Infrastructure Requirements

- **Scalable Data Storage**: Systems capable of managing continuous data streams from thousands of patients
- **Interoperability Standards**: FHIR-based APIs enabling standardized device data integration
- **Security Architecture**: End-to-end encryption protecting sensitive information throughout transmission

Patient Engagement Strategies

- **Technology Selection Guidance**: Helping patients choose appropriate monitoring devices

- **Data Interpretation Education**: Teaching patients to understand and act on their own health data
- **Sustained Engagement Approaches**: Behavioral techniques supporting long-term monitoring adherence

Future Directions in Connected Health

Emerging trends will further transform wearable integration with EHRs:

- **Passive Monitoring Technologies**: Sensors embedded in clothing, furniture, and environments gathering data without active user engagement
- **Advanced Physiological Sensing**: Next-generation wearables monitoring blood pressure, glucose, and other biomarkers non-invasively
- **Closed-Loop Systems**: Automated response systems adjusting treatments based on real-time monitoring data

10.4 Preparing for the Future of Personalized Medicine and Patient-Centric Care

The healthcare ecosystem is evolving toward increasingly personalized approaches tailored to individual patient characteristics. Building on the patient engagement frameworks discussed in Chapter 5 and the data-driven strategies explored in Chapters 7 and 8, organizations must prepare for this fundamental transformation.

The Foundations of Personalized Medicine

Personalized medicine leverages comprehensive individual data to customize prevention, diagnosis, and treatment:

- **Genomic Information**: DNA sequencing identifying disease risks and treatment response predictors
- **Longitudinal Health Data**: Comprehensive health histories revealing patterns and trajectories
- **Environmental Context**: Understanding how living conditions and exposures affect health
- **Behavioral Patterns**: Recognition of individual lifestyle factors influencing outcomes
- **Patient Preferences**: Incorporation of personal values and priorities into care decisions

Organizational Readiness Framework for Personalized Medicine

Capability Domain	Current State Assessment Questions	Future State Requirements	Implementation Priorities
Data Infra-structure	• Can we integrate genetic, clinical and lifestyle data? • Do we have systems for longitudinal data analysis? • How accessible is our data for precision analytics?	• Comprehensive data integration platform • Longitudinal patient record architecture • Advanced analytics capabilities	• Data lake implementation • Genomic data integration • FHIR-based interoperability
Clinical Integration	• How do clinicians access precision medicine tools? • Are workflows optimized for personalized care? • What decision support exists for genomic medicine?	• Point-of-care genomic information • Personalized risk calculation tools • Integrated decision support	• Clinician education programs • Workflow redesign • Genomic CDS implementation
Patient Engage-ment	• How do patients access their precision health data? • Can patients contribute self-generated health data? • How are preferences incorporated into care plans?	• Intuitive genomic results interfaces • Patient-reported outcome platforms • Preference documentation tools	• Patient portal enhancement • Health literacy programs • Digital engagement strategies
Gover-nance & Ethics	• What oversight exists for precision medicine? • How are equity concerns addressed? • What consent processes are implemented?	• Multidisciplinary governance committee • Health equity monitoring system • Dynamic consent management	• Ethics committee formation • Disparities monitoring • Consent process redesign

FIGURE 10.7: Organizational Readiness Assessment for Personalized Medicine.

Technological Enablers of Personalized Care

Several emerging technologies support the transition to personalized medicine:

Advanced Genomics and Multi-Omics Integration

Building on the data types discussed in Chapter 2, EHRs will increasingly incorporate complex molecular information:

- **Whole Genome Sequencing**: Comprehensive DNA analysis identifying disease risks and treatment response predictors
- **Pharmacogenomics**: Genetic testing revealing how individuals metabolize medications
- **Transcriptomics**: RNA analysis showing which genes are actively expressed
- **Proteomics and Metabolomics**: Protein and metabolite profiling providing functional insights

Example: An integrated EHR system automatically incorporates pharmacogenomic data to guide medication selection and dosing, alerting clinicians when a patient's genetic profile suggests altered metabolism of prescribed drugs.

Artificial Intelligence for Precision Therapeutics

As explored earlier in this chapter, AI capabilities enable truly personalized treatment approaches:

- **Treatment Response Prediction**: Algorithms forecasting individual outcomes across treatment options
- **Optimal Therapy Selection**: AI-driven analysis identifying the most effective intervention for specific patient profiles
- **Dosing Optimization**: Precision adjustment of medication dosages based on individual characteristics

Example: An oncology AI system analyzes a cancer patient's tumor genetic profile, past treatment responses, and thousands of similar cases to recommend the optimal personalized treatment protocol with the highest probability of response.

Patient-Centered Digital Ecosystems

Next-generation digital platforms will support personalized care delivery:

- **Comprehensive Patient Portals**: Integrated systems providing access to personal health information, educational resources, and care team communication

- **Custom Health Applications**: Personalized mobile tools tailored to individual health needs and goals
- **Virtual Care Platforms**: Telehealth systems enabling convenient access to personalized guidance

Example: A diabetes management platform integrates continuous glucose monitoring data, nutritional information, medication tracking, and personalized AI coaching to create an individualized management program optimized for each patient's specific needs and lifestyle.

Evolving Care Models for Personalized Medicine

Healthcare delivery models must transform to support personalized approaches:

Value-Based Care Alignment

As introduced in Chapter 9, value-based models create financial alignment with personalized care:

- **Outcome-Based Reimbursement**: Payment systems rewarding improved health outcomes rather than service volume
- **Risk Stratification**: Population segmentation enabling targeted resource allocation
- **Prevention Incentives**: Financial models supporting proactive intervention before disease progression

Example: An accountable care organization implements precision risk stratification, identifying patients most likely to benefit from intensive management programs and allocating resources accordingly.

Shared Decision-Making Implementation

Personalized medicine requires collaborative decision processes:

- **Patient Preference Elicitation**: Structured approaches to understanding individual priorities and values
- **Personalized Risk Communication**: Tailored presentation of health risks and treatment benefits
- **Decision Aid Development**: Tools helping patients understand complex medical choices

Example: A surgical decision support system presents personalized risk calculations based on a patient's specific characteristics, helping them understand their individual likelihood of complications and expected outcomes.

Team-Based Care Coordination

Complex personalized care requires coordinated multidisciplinary approaches:

- **Care Team Communication Platforms**: Systems enabling seamless information sharing across team members
- **Role Optimization**: Task distribution matching team member skills with patient needs
- **Longitudinal Relationship Management**: Structures supporting continuous healing relationships

Example: A complex care platform coordinates services across primary care, specialists, pharmacists, and community resources, with AI assistance prioritizing interventions based on each patient's unique needs and preferences.

Implementation Roadmap for Personalized Medicine

Organizations can follow a phased approach to personalized medicine implementation:

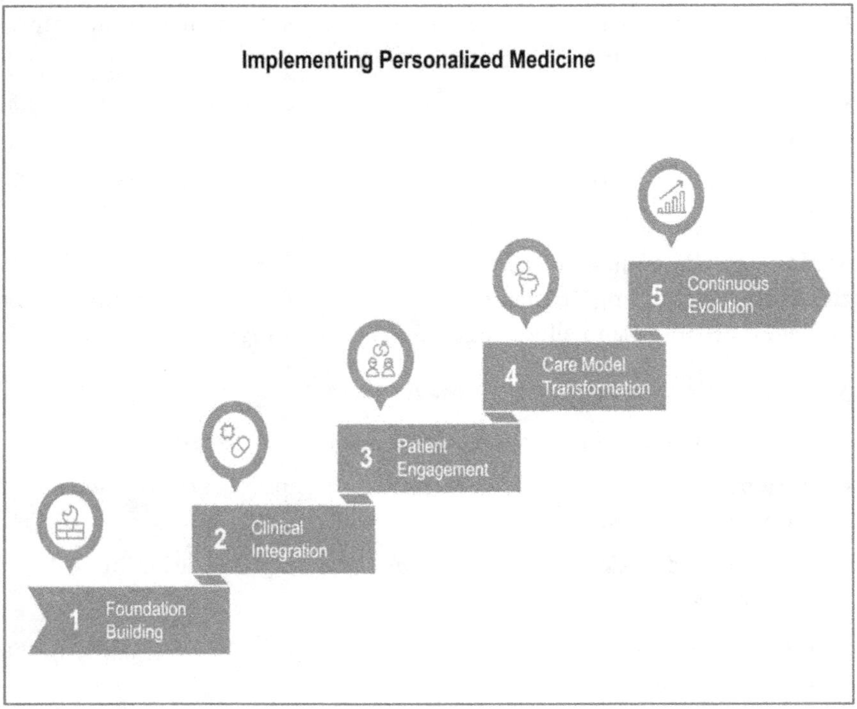

FIGURE 10.8: Personalized Medicine Implementation Roadmap.

How EHRs Will Evolve Over the Next 10 Years

Looking beyond current capabilities, the next decade will bring transformative changes to EHR systems. While previous chapters examined today's state-of-the-art, this section explores the horizon of healthcare information technology through 2030 and beyond.

1. **AI-Powered Predictive Analytics:** Building on the AI foundation discussed earlier in this chapter:

   - **Real-Time Risk Assessment**: AI systems will continuously analyze patient data streams to identify subtle signals preceding disease development
   - **Individualized Prevention Strategies**: Predictive models will generate personalized recommendations for disease prevention based on comprehensive risk profiles
   - **Treatment Optimization Algorithms**: AI will predict treatment responses across options, enabling precision therapy selection

   Future Impact: These capabilities will fundamentally shift healthcare from reactive treatment to proactive prevention, identifying high-risk individuals years before clinical manifestation of disease.

2. **Universal Interoperability Standards:** Expanding on the interoperability challenges discussed in Chapter 2:

   - **Global FHIR Implementation**: Fast Healthcare Interoperability Resources will achieve worldwide adoption, ensuring standardized data exchange
   - **Universal Patient Identifiers**: Secure, privacy-protecting identification systems will resolve current patient matching challenges
   - **Cross-Border Health Information Exchange**: International standards will enable seamless medical record portability across healthcare systems globally

   Future Impact: True interoperability will eliminate care fragmentation, reduce duplicate testing and medical errors, and create unprecedented continuity across health systems.

3. **Blockchain-Secured Patient Data Control:** Building on the blockchain fundamentals explored earlier in this chapter:

   - **Patient-Owned Health Records**: Individuals will control their comprehensive health data through blockchain-based personal health records

- **Granular Permission Management**: Smart contracts will enable patients to grant specific, time-limited access rights to selected providers
- **Immutable Audit Trails**: Complete, tamper-proof documentation of all data access will ensure accountability

Future Impact: Blockchain will revolutionize health data ownership, shifting control from institutions to individuals while dramatically enhancing security.

4. **AI-Powered Clinical Assistants:** Advancing beyond current documentation tools:
    - **Ambient Clinical Intelligence**: Voice-enabled systems will automatically document patient encounters without physician data entry
    - **Virtual Clinical Advisors**: AI assistants will offer real-time guidance during patient care, suggesting questions, diagnostics, and treatments
    - **Automated Documentation Review**: AI will analyze clinical notes to identify missing information and potential errors

    Future Impact: These technologies will dramatically reduce administrative burden, allowing clinicians to focus on human aspects of patient care.

5. **Continuous Monitoring Integration:** Expanding on the wearable integration discussed earlier:
    - **Passive Monitoring Ecosystems**: Networks of environmental sensors will supplement wearables, creating comprehensive monitoring without patient effort
    - **Closed-Loop Intervention Systems**: Monitoring data will trigger automated interventions ranging from medication adjustments to emergency responses
    - **Digital Biomarker Development**: Novel measurements from consumer devices will be validated as clinical indicators

    Future Impact: The distinction between clinical and daily life will blur as healthcare becomes a continuous process rather than episodic interactions.

6. **Decentralized Health Data Networks:** Building on the interoperability discussion from Chapter 2:
    - **Federated Learning Systems**: AI will analyze distributed datasets without centralizing sensitive information
    - **Patient-Controlled Data Sharing**: Individuals will selectively contribute their data to research through secure privacy-preserving mechanisms

- **Distributed Research Networks**: Large-scale studies will occur across institutional boundaries with unprecedented scale and diversity

Future Impact: These networks will accelerate medical discovery while enhancing privacy protection, enabling research that was previously impossible.

The Future EHR Experience: A Comparative View

Stake-holder	Current EHR Experience (2023)	Future EHR Experience (2030+)
Patients	• Limited portal access to records • Basic appointment scheduling • Simple secure messaging • Fragmented records across systems	• Complete health data ownership • AI health assistants providing guidance • Continuous monitoring integration • Seamless access across all providers
Physi-cians	• Significant documentation burden • Basic clinical decision support • Limited predictive capabilities • Workflow disruptions	• Ambient documentation through voice • Advanced AI diagnostic assistance • Predictive intervention recommendations • Optimized workflows reducing burden
Health Systems	• Siloed data repositories • Limited interoperability • Reactive care models • Basic population analytics	• Connected care networks • Seamless data exchange • Proactive prevention models • AI-powered resource optimization
Resear-chers	• Complex data access processes • Limited dataset size and diversity • Privacy challenges limiting studies • Significant data cleaning requirements	• Privacy-preserving distributed analysis • Massive diverse research datasets • Patient-controlled data contribution • Real-time insights from live data
Payers	• Delayed claims processing • Limited outcome visibility • Retrospective utilization review • Broad risk assessment	• Real-time claims adjudication • Continuous outcome monitoring • Predictive utilization management • Precision risk stratification

FIGURE 10.9: Evolution of EHR Experience by Stakeholder.

The Great Debate: AI in Healthcare—Revolution or Risk?

As artificial intelligence increasingly integrates into EHR systems and clinical workflows, a robust debate has emerged among healthcare leaders, ethicists, technologists, and patient advocates. This debate centers on a fundamental question: Does machine learning-driven healthcare represent a transformative advancement that will dramatically improve outcomes, or does it introduce new risks that could undermine care quality and patient trust?

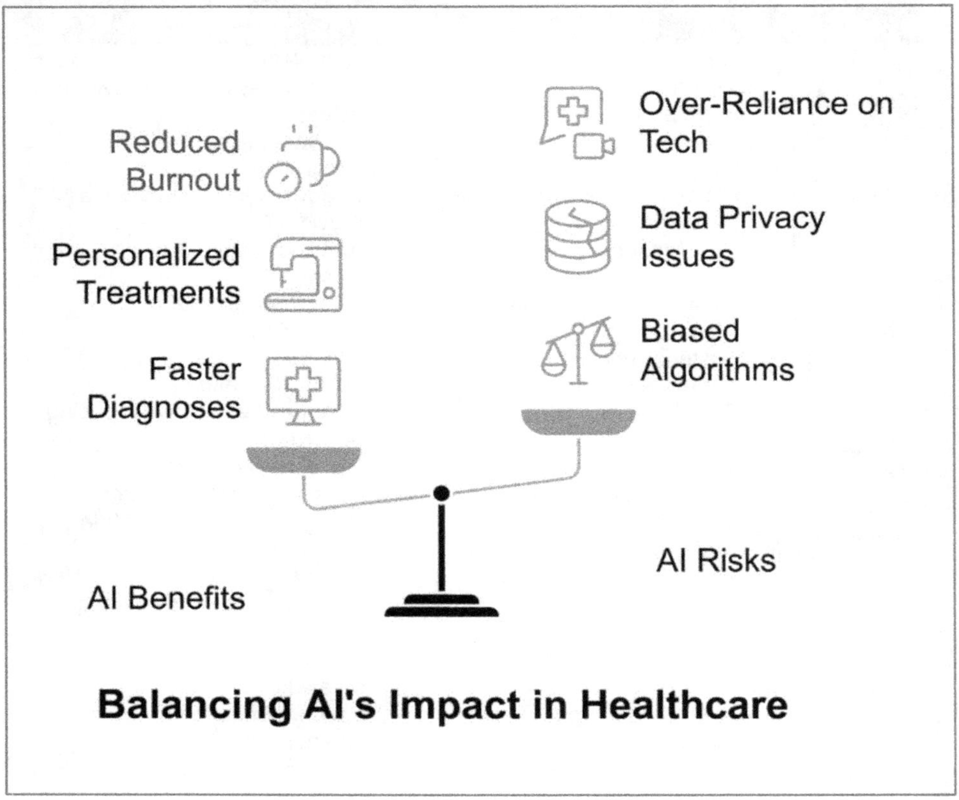

FIGURE 10.10: Balancing AI's Impact in Healthcare.

Proponents: AI as a Healthcare Game-Changer

Leading AI advocates highlight several transformative capabilities that could fundamentally reshape healthcare delivery:

Enhanced Diagnostic Accuracy and Early Detection

AI systems can process millions of data points instantaneously, identifying subtle patterns that human clinicians might miss. This capability extends across numerous domains:

- **Medical Imaging**: AI algorithms have demonstrated remarkable accuracy in detecting malignancies in radiological images, often identifying cancers at earlier stages than human radiologists
- **Laboratory Test Interpretation**: Machine learning models can identify subtle patterns across laboratory values that predict disease development before clinical symptoms appear
- **Physiological Monitoring**: AI analysis of continuous monitoring data can detect deterioration patterns hours before conventional clinical signs emerge

Real-World Impact: A 2023 multi-center study published in *Nature Medicine* demonstrated that an AI system analyzing retinal images could detect early signs of diabetic retinopathy with 97.5% sensitivity, while simultaneously identifying biomarkers for cardiovascular disease and neurological conditions—all from a single retinal scan. This enabled preventive interventions years before clinical manifestation of symptoms.

Personalized Treatment Optimization

AI enables unprecedented treatment personalization through sophisticated analysis of individual characteristics:

- **Pharmacogenomic Matching**: Algorithms can predict medication responses based on genetic profiles, ensuring patients receive therapeutics most likely to be effective for their specific genetic makeup
- **Multi-factor Treatment Selection**: Machine learning models can integrate genomic, clinical, social, and environmental data to identify optimal individualized treatment approaches
- **Dynamic Therapy Adjustment**: AI can continuously monitor treatment responses and recommend real-time modifications to optimize outcomes

Real-World Impact: The Mayo Clinic implemented an AI-powered oncology platform that analyzes a patient's comprehensive tumor genetic profile alongside their medical history, comparing results with millions of similar cases to recommend personalized treatment protocols. In a clinical validation study, patients receiving AI-recommended treatments showed a 27% improvement in progression-free survival compared to standard care pathways.

Reduced Clinician Burden and Burnout

Healthcare professionals face unprecedented administrative burdens contributing to widespread burnout. AI offers several solutions:

- **Automated Documentation**: Natural language processing can generate structured clinical notes from patient encounters without manual data entry
- **Workflow Optimization**: AI systems can intelligently prioritize tasks, notifications, and information based on clinical relevance
- **Administrative Automation**: Machine learning can handle routine administrative tasks like prior authorization, appointment scheduling, and routine communication

Real-World Impact: Providence Health implemented an AI documentation assistant that listens during patient encounters and automatically generates structured clinical notes while identifying potential gaps in documentation. Physicians reported a 72% reduction in documentation time and significantly improved work satisfaction scores within six months of implementation.

Population Health Management and Health Equity

AI brings unprecedented capabilities for understanding and addressing population-level health challenges:

- **Social Determinant Analysis**: Machine learning can identify patterns linking social factors to health outcomes across diverse communities
- **Resource Allocation Optimization**: AI models can predict community-level health needs to guide more equitable resource distribution
- **Proactive Outreach Targeting**: Analytics can identify high-risk individuals who would benefit from preventive interventions

Real-World Impact: Boston Medical Center deployed an AI-driven population health platform that analyzes comprehensive EHR data alongside social determinant information to identify patients at highest risk for preventable hospitalizations. The system has enabled targeted interventions that reduced admission rates by 31% in previously underserved communities.

Skeptics: The Risks of AI in Healthcare

Critics raise legitimate concerns about AI implementation in healthcare environments:

Algorithmic Bias and Health Disparities

AI systems reflect the data used to train them, potentially perpetuating or amplifying existing biases:

- **Training Data Limitations**: Historically marginalized populations are often underrepresented in healthcare datasets
- **Performance Disparities**: Studies show some AI systems perform differently across demographic groups, potentially exacerbating healthcare inequities
- **Embedded Historical Bias**: Algorithms trained on historical data may incorporate and propagate existing patterns of healthcare discrimination

Real-World Example: A widely-deployed algorithm used to identify patients for enhanced care management programs was found to systematically underestimate the needs of Black patients. The algorithm used healthcare costs as a proxy for health needs, but failed to account for historical patterns of reduced healthcare access and utilization among Black populations. When researchers recalibrated the algorithm to focus on medical conditions rather than costs, the racial bias was significantly reduced.

Data Privacy, Security, and Consent Concerns

AI healthcare applications introduce novel privacy considerations:

- **Comprehensive Data Requirements**: Advanced AI models often require massive datasets containing sensitive health information
- **Re-identification Risks**: Complex AI systems may inadvertently enable re-identification of supposedly anonymized data
- **Secondary Use Questions**: Patients may not anticipate how their data might inform future AI applications

Real-World Example: In 2019, a major health system partnered with a technology company to develop an AI diagnostic tool without specifically informing patients that their data would be used for this purpose. When publicly revealed, the arrangement sparked significant controversy about proper consent for AI development using patient data, leading to regulatory investigations and policy changes.

Over-Reliance and Automation Complacency

The psychological impact of AI systems on clinical decision-making raises important concerns:

- **Automation Bias**: Clinicians may over-rely on AI recommendations, accepting them without appropriate critical evaluation
- **Skill Erosion**: Excessive reliance on AI systems could potentially erode clinical reasoning skills over time
- **Accountability Questions**: When AI significantly influences clinical decisions, questions emerge about responsibility for outcomes

Real-World Example: A study published in *JAMA Internal Medicine* found that when presented with AI diagnostic suggestions, physicians were 26% less likely to consider alternative diagnoses not suggested by the AI, even when clinical evidence supported these alternatives. This raises concerns about automation bias potentially narrowing clinical thinking.

The Risk of Dehumanizing Healthcare

Perhaps the most fundamental concern involves the potential impact on the human dimensions of healthcare:

- **Reduced Human Interaction**: Over-reliance on technology might diminish the essential human connection between providers and patients
- **Empathy Limitations**: AI systems cannot truly understand patient experiences, potentially undermining compassionate care
- **Contextual Understanding Gaps**: Algorithms may miss critical psychosocial and cultural contexts that human providers instinctively incorporate

Real-World **Example**: A survey of patients at facilities using AI-driven triage and initial assessment systems reported a 34% reduction in perceived provider empathy compared to traditional care models. Patients expressed concern that their unique circumstances and concerns were being reduced to data points rather than fully understood.

Navigating the Middle Path: Toward Responsible AI Implementation

A nuanced approach recognizes both the transformative potential and genuine risks of healthcare AI. Leading organizations are developing frameworks for responsible implementation:

Core Principles for Ethical Healthcare AI

Several fundamental principles can guide responsible deployment:

Principle	Implementation Approach	Example
Human Oversight	Maintain human clinician review of critical AI recommendations	Mayo Clinic's "Human in the Loop" model requires physician confirmation of all AI diagnostic recommendations before clinical action
Algorithmic Transparency	Prioritize explainable AI allowing clinicians to understand recommendation rationales	Beth Israel Deaconess Medical Center implemented an explainable AI system that provides visualization of the specific findings influencing its diagnostic suggestions
Inclusive Development	Ensure diverse participation in AI development, validation, and governance	Intermountain Healthcare established a diverse AI ethics committee including clinicians, patients, ethicists, and community representatives from varied backgrounds
Rigorous Validation	Test AI performance across diverse populations before deployment	Duke Health implemented a validation protocol requiring demonstration of consistent AI performance across different demographic groups before clinical implementation
Continuous Monitoring	Establish ongoing surveillance for unexpected behaviors or disparate impacts	University of California Health developed an AI monitoring system that continuously analyzes for performance variations across patient populations
Patient Autonomy	Ensure patients understand when AI influences their care	Cleveland Clinic implemented a transparency policy requiring disclosure to patients when AI significantly influences their diagnosis or treatment

FIGURE 10.11: Ethical Principles for Healthcare AI Implementation.

Regulators' Evolving Approach

Regulatory frameworks are adapting to address the unique challenges of healthcare AI:

- **FDA's New Paradigm**: The FDA has developed the Software Pre-Certification Program specifically addressing the iterative nature of AI/ML-based software as a medical device
- **Algorithmic Impact Assessments**: Several jurisdictions now require formal assessment of potential algorithm impacts before healthcare deployment
- **Ongoing Validation Requirements**: Emerging regulations require continuous performance monitoring rather than just pre-market approval

The Clinician's Perspective

Healthcare professionals on the frontlines offer valuable insights on effective AI integration:

"The most successful AI implementations in our system have been those designed with clinicians as partners from the beginning—where the technology truly addresses our pain points rather than creating new workflows. When AI reduces administrative burden and helps me make better decisions for my patients, it's transformative. But it must complement rather than attempt to replace clinical judgment."

— Dr. Sarah Michaels, Chief Medical Information Officer, Northwestern Medicine

The Patient's Voice

Patient advocates emphasize the importance of maintaining human connection:

"I want my doctors to use every tool available, including AI, to help me get the best care possible. But I also need to know they're really seeing me as a person, not just a collection of data points. The challenge is finding that balance where technology enhances rather than replaces the human relationship at the heart of healthcare."

— Michael Rodriguez, Patient Advocate, National Patient Partnership Council

Toward an Integrated Vision

The most promising future lies not in choosing between technology and humanity, but in thoughtfully integrating them:

- **Augmentation, Not Replacement**: Position AI as enhancing human capabilities rather than replacing human judgment
- **Collaborative Intelligence**: Design systems where humans and AI contribute their complementary strengths
- **Values-Based Implementation**: Ensure technology deployment reflects core healthcare values—beneficence, non-maleficence, justice, and autonomy
- **Inclusive Governance**: Involve diverse stakeholders in ongoing oversight of healthcare AI systems

The transformative potential of AI in healthcare is undeniable, but realizing this potential while mitigating risks requires thoughtful implementation guided by strong ethical principles, inclusive governance, and a commitment to preserving the essential human dimensions of healthcare.

As one healthcare leader aptly summarized: "The question isn't whether AI will transform healthcare—it's whether we'll harness its power wisely to create a healthcare system that's both more capable and more humane than what we have today."

Final Thoughts: The Future of EHRs, AI, and Connected Healthcare

The evolution of Electronic Health Records will fundamentally transform healthcare delivery over the coming decade. Building on the foundation established in earlier chapters, several key themes will shape this future:

Strategic Integration of Emerging Technologies

The most successful healthcare organizations will thoughtfully integrate emerging technologies while maintaining focus on core clinical missions:

- **AI Enhancement**: Artificial intelligence will increasingly augment clinical decision-making, administrative processes, and patient engagement
- **Blockchain Security**: Distributed ledger technologies will revolutionize health data ownership, control, and security
- **Ubiquitous Monitoring**: The boundaries between clinical and daily environments will blur as continuous monitoring becomes standard
- **Intelligent Automation**: Routine cognitive tasks will be increasingly handled by AI systems, allowing humans to focus on high-value activities

The Shift to Truly Patient-Centered Care

As discussed throughout this book, technology will enable a fundamental reorientation toward genuine patient-centeredness:

- **Patient Data Ownership**: Individuals will control their comprehensive health records with granular permission management
- **Personalized Medicine**: Treatments will be increasingly tailored to individual characteristics and preferences
- **Continuous Engagement**: Care will extend beyond episodic visits to ongoing relationships supported by digital tools
- **Empowered Self-Management**: Patients will have unprecedented ability to understand and manage their own health

Addressing Emerging Ethical Challenges

New technologies bring novel ethical considerations requiring proactive attention:

- **Algorithmic Fairness**: Ensuring AI systems perform equitably across all patient populations
- **Privacy Protection**: Developing frameworks balancing data utilization with individual privacy rights
- **Digital Divide Mitigation**: Preventing technological advancement from exacerbating healthcare disparities
- **Human-Technology Balance**: Maintaining the essential human elements of healthcare while leveraging technology

The healthcare organizations that most effectively navigate these opportunities and challenges will lead the transformation toward an intelligent, connected healthcare ecosystem that delivers unprecedented clinical outcomes while enhancing the human experience of both providing and receiving care.

As we conclude this exploration of EHRs and pharmaceutical marketing, it's clear that we stand at an inflection point in healthcare's evolution. The technologies, strategies, and frameworks discussed throughout this book provide a roadmap for harnessing the power of health information to improve clinical outcomes, enhance patient experiences, and optimize resource utilization across the healthcare ecosystem.

Chapter Eleven

Ethical Considerations & The Future of EHRs in Pharma

Balancing Innovation with Responsibility

As Electronic Health Records continue to evolve from the basic digital systems described in Chapter 1 to the sophisticated AI-enhanced platforms explored in Chapter 10, stakeholders across the healthcare ecosystem face increasingly complex ethical challenges. While previous chapters have examined the technical capabilities, strategic applications, and regulatory requirements of EHR systems, this chapter focuses specifically on the ethical dimensions that must guide responsible implementation.

From patient privacy concerns to the responsible use of AI-driven analytics, ensuring ethical compliance is paramount when leveraging EHR data for pharmaceutical marketing, research, and patient care. This final chapter explores the ethical imperatives that will shape the future of healthcare information technology.

This chapter explores:

- The fundamental ethical dilemmas surrounding EHR data utilization in pharmaceutical marketing and research
- Evidence-based case studies demonstrating ethical best practices in real-world scenarios
- Strategic frameworks for maintaining compliance while building public trust
- Emerging trends that will shape the ethical landscape of EHR systems in the coming decade

The Ethical Foundation of Healthcare Data Utilization

As discussed throughout this book, EHRs contain extraordinarily sensitive information requiring careful ethical consideration. Building on the security frameworks outlined in Chapter 3 and the regulatory requirements detailed in Chapter 6, this section examines the core ethical principles that should guide all EHR implementations.

Core Ethical Principles for EHR Utilization

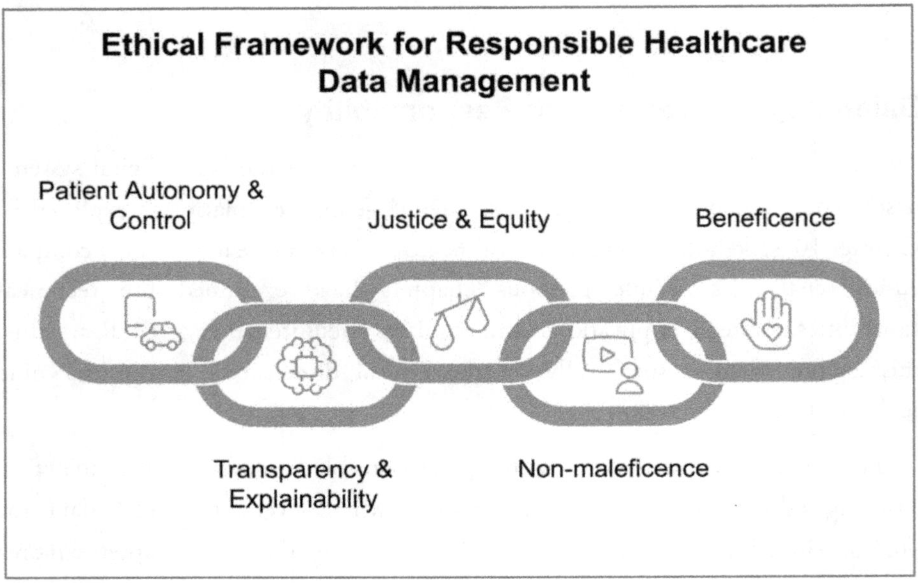

FIGURE 11.1: Core Ethical Principles for Healthcare Data Utilization.

Patient Autonomy and Data Control

Building on the patient engagement concepts introduced in Chapter 5, respecting individual autonomy requires:

- **Informed Consent**: Patients must understand how their data will be used and have meaningful choices about participation
- **Granular Permission Management**: Providing individuals with specific control over different data types and uses
- **Right to Access and Amendment**: Ensuring patients can view their own information and correct inaccuracies

Key Consideration: The technical capabilities for patient data control discussed in Chapter 10 must be guided by ethical frameworks that genuinely respect individual autonomy rather than creating an illusion of control through complex permission systems.

Transparency and Explainability

As AI systems increasingly influence healthcare decisions (explored in Chapter 10), transparency becomes essential:

- **Algorithm Transparency**: Healthcare stakeholders should understand how AI systems analyze data and reach conclusions
- **Plain Language Communication**: Complex data practices must be explained in accessible terminology
- **Process Visibility**: Creating clear audit trails showing how data influences decisions

Key Consideration: Beyond regulatory compliance discussed in Chapter 6, organizations must develop genuine transparency practices that enable meaningful understanding by patients and providers.

Justice and Equity

The digital transformation of healthcare creates both opportunities and risks for health equity:

- **Accessibility Requirements**: Ensuring EHR benefits extend to all patients regardless of technical literacy, language, or disability
- **Algorithmic Fairness**: Preventing AI systems from perpetuating or amplifying existing healthcare disparities
- **Representative Data**: Ensuring systems are trained and validated on diverse populations

Key Consideration: As discussed in Chapter 10's expanded section on AI ethics, technology implementations must explicitly address equity concerns rather than assuming neutral impact.

Key Ethical Considerations in EHR Utilization

Building on the fundamental principles, several specific ethical considerations deserve focused attention:

Data Privacy and Security

As examined in Chapter 3, robust privacy and security measures form the foundation of ethical EHR utilization:

- **Beyond Minimum Compliance**: Ethical organizations exceed baseline regulatory requirements outlined in Chapter 6
- **Contextual Integrity**: Respecting appropriate information flows based on context and relationships
- **Privacy by Design**: Building privacy protections into systems from inception rather than adding them later

Key Evolution: The transition from traditional security models to blockchain-based patient-controlled systems described in Chapter 10 represents a significant ethical advancement by aligning technological capabilities with core ethical principles.

Algorithmic Bias and Fairness

The AI capabilities explored in Chapter 10 introduce complex ethical considerations:

- **Representative Training Data**: Ensuring AI systems learn from diverse patient populations
- **Fairness Metrics**: Implementing specific measures to detect and mitigate bias
- **Human Oversight**: Maintaining appropriate clinical judgment in AI-augmented decision processes

Key Insight: The expanded discussion of healthcare AI in Chapter 10 highlighted that addressing algorithmic bias requires both technical solutions and governance frameworks that prioritize equity.

Digital Divide and Access Equity

The patient engagement technologies discussed in Chapter 5 must be implemented with equity considerations:

- **Universal Design Principles**: Creating systems usable across varying technical abilities
- **Accessibility Requirements**: Ensuring accommodation for users with disabilities

- **Language and Cultural Considerations**: Supporting diverse patient populations

Key Challenge: The sophisticated technologies described in Chapter 10 risk exacerbating healthcare disparities unless explicitly designed for equitable access.

Case Study: How Roche Ensured Ethical Compliance in Real-World Evidence (RWE) Studies

The Challenge: Balancing Research Value with Patient Privacy

Roche sought to leverage EHR-derived real-world evidence to enhance drug safety monitoring and treatment optimization—capabilities discussed in Chapter 4. However, the company faced significant challenges in collecting and analyzing this data while maintaining ethical standards and regulatory compliance outlined in Chapter 6.

Strategic Solution: Privacy-Preserving Technology and Governance

To maintain ethical compliance while achieving research objectives, Roche implemented a comprehensive approach:

- **Federated Learning Architecture**: Rather than centralizing sensitive data, AI models were deployed to analyze de-identified patient information on hospital servers, with only the learning algorithms—not patient data—traveling between systems
- **Blockchain-Based Consent Management**: Building on the blockchain concepts explored in Chapter 10, Roche implemented a secure system allowing patients to review and control how their data was used for research purposes
- **Independent Ethics Review Board (ERB)**: A third-party ethics panel with diverse membership provided ongoing oversight ensuring HIPAA and GDPR compliance while evaluating potential ethical implications of research methods

Measurable Outcomes

The initiative delivered significant benefits while maintaining ethical standards:

- Researchers accessed valuable real-world evidence without compromising patient privacy
- The company avoided regulatory scrutiny by proactively addressing ethical concerns before they emerged
- The approach established Roche as an industry leader in ethical EHR-based research methodologies

Contd...

Key Implementation Insights

- Ethical EHR utilization can simultaneously drive pharmaceutical innovation and maintain patient trust
- Privacy-preserving technologies like federated learning enable large-scale research without compromising individual privacy
- Independent oversight and transparency are essential elements of responsible data governance

Source: Roche AI-Powered RWE Compliance Report (2022)

Ethical Best Practices Across the Healthcare Ecosystem

Different stakeholders in the healthcare ecosystem have distinct ethical responsibilities when utilizing EHR data:

For Healthcare Providers

Building on the implementation considerations discussed in Chapter 9:

- **Meaningful Consent Processes**: Develop genuinely informative consent procedures beyond minimal compliance
- **Transparent Data Governance**: Establish clear data-sharing policies with explicit privacy safeguards
- **Comprehensive Security Implementation**: Deploy robust measures preventing unauthorized data access
- **Equity-Focused Implementation**: Ensure EHR benefits extend across all patient populations

For Pharmaceutical Organizations

Extending the marketing frameworks outlined in Chapters 7 and 8:

- **De-Identification Standards**: Implement rigorous protocols exceeding minimum requirements for data anonymization
- **Bias Prevention Methodology**: Validate AI models against diverse populations to prevent algorithmic discrimination
- **Clear Purpose Limitation**: Establish explicit boundaries around appropriate data utilization
- **Transparent Provider Engagement**: Maintain openness with healthcare providers about how data-driven insights influence engagement

For Technology Developers

Building on the emerging technologies discussed in Chapter 10:

- **Ethics-by-Design Approaches**: Integrate ethical considerations from the earliest development stages
- **Inclusive Development Practices**: Ensure diverse representation in technology creation
- **Explainable AI Implementation**: Develop systems whose recommend-dations can be understood by clinicians and patients
- **Continuous Ethical Evaluation**: Implement ongoing monitoring for unintended consequences

The Great Debate: Should Pharmaceutical Companies Have Access to EHR Data?

The question of whether pharmaceutical companies should access EHR data represents one of the most contested ethical issues in healthcare. This debate extends beyond the technical capabilities explored in Chapters 7 and 8 to fundamental questions about appropriate data stewardship.

Argument For: EHR Data Improves Drug Development & Patient Outcomes

Proponents emphasize several potential benefits to patients and healthcare systems:

1. **Accelerated Therapeutic Development**
   - Real-world data enables more efficient clinical trial recruitment and design
   - EHR insights help identify unmet medical needs that might otherwise remain unaddressed
   - Diverse real-world patient data supplements limited clinical trial populations

   Example: In 2022, a pharmaceutical company analyzed de-identified EHR data to identify a rare neurological condition subtype responsive to an existing therapy, leading to a successful targeted clinical trial and new treatment option for previously untreatable patients.

2. **Enhanced Post-Market Safety Surveillance**
    - EHR data enables detection of adverse drug reactions not identified in clinical trials
    - Comprehensive real-world monitoring improves therapy safety profiles over time
    - Population-scale analysis identifies rare side effects that wouldn't appear in limited trials

    Example: Analysis of EHR data from millions of patients revealed a previously undetected cardiovascular risk associated with a widely-prescribed diabetes medication, enabling updated safety labeling and appropriate monitoring that potentially prevented thousands of adverse events.

3. **Precision Medicine Advancement**
    - EHR insights facilitate identification of specific patient subgroups most likely to benefit from therapies
    - Real-world effectiveness data helps optimize treatment selection for individual patients
    - Comprehensive health histories enable better prediction of therapeutic responses

    Example: By analyzing de-identified EHR data, researchers discovered that patients with a specific genetic biomarker showed significantly better responses to a particular cancer immunotherapy, enabling more precise treatment selection and improving outcomes.

Argument Against: Privacy & Ethical Risks Outweigh Potential Benefits

Critics highlight several significant concerns regarding pharmaceutical access to EHR data:

Potential for Data Misuse

- Commercial interests might prioritize profitable treatment pathways over patient-centered approaches
- Patients rarely understand how their health data might be monetized by third parties

- Limited transparency about how insights influence marketing and research priorities

Example: An investigation revealed a pharmaceutical company used EHR-derived insights to specifically target marketing efforts toward physicians with patients likely to be profitable long-term customers, rather than those most likely to benefit clinically.

Risk of Algorithmic Bias in Insights

- AI models trained on biased healthcare data may perpetuate or amplify existing disparities
- Historical inequities in healthcare access create datasets that underrepresent marginalized populations
- Commercial incentives may not prioritize equitable algorithm development

Example: An AI system analyzing EHR data to identify candidates for a clinical trial systematically underidentified eligible Black patients due to historical patterns of underdiagnosis and undertesting reflected in the training data.

Insufficient Patient Control and Transparency

- Current models often provide limited patient visibility into how their data influences pharmaceutical activities
- Informed consent processes rarely explain commercial uses in accessible language
- Few mechanisms exist for patients to monitor or limit specific data uses

Example: Surveys reveal that while over 80% of patients believe they should control how their health data is used, fewer than 15% could accurately describe how de-identified data flows to commercial entities under current practices.

Finding Common Ground: A Balanced Approach

Several core principles can help balance innovation and ethical responsibility:

- **Meaningful Consent Frameworks**: Developing genuinely informative consent models giving patients real control
- **Independent Governance Structures**: Establishing oversight committees with diverse stakeholder representation including patients
- **Outcome-Based Evaluation**: Measuring success by patient health improvements rather than commercial metrics alone

- **Transparency Requirements**: Creating clear disclosure about how pharmaceutical companies use de-identified data
- **Equity Monitoring Systems**: Implementing ongoing assessment of whether benefits extend across all patient populations

11.1 Navigating Evolving Privacy Regulations and Data Governance Frameworks

The Dynamic Regulatory Landscape

Building on the compliance frameworks outlined in Chapter 6, healthcare organizations must navigate an increasingly complex regulatory environment governing EHR data. This landscape continues to evolve in response to technological advancements, changing public expectations, and emerging ethical concerns.

Current Regulatory Foundations

- **HIPAA Evolution**: The Health Insurance Portability and Accountability Act remains the cornerstone of U.S. healthcare privacy regulation, but interpretations and enforcement continue to evolve
- **State-Level Initiatives**: Many states have enacted additional privacy laws with requirements that exceed federal standards
- **International Frameworks**: Global organizations must navigate varying international approaches including GDPR in Europe

Implementation Example: A multi-state healthcare system implemented a regulatory tracking system that automatically identifies which state and federal regulations apply to each facility, ensuring compliance with the strictest applicable standards in each location.

Comprehensive Data Governance Implementation

Effective data governance extends beyond regulatory compliance to encompass ethical principles and organizational values:

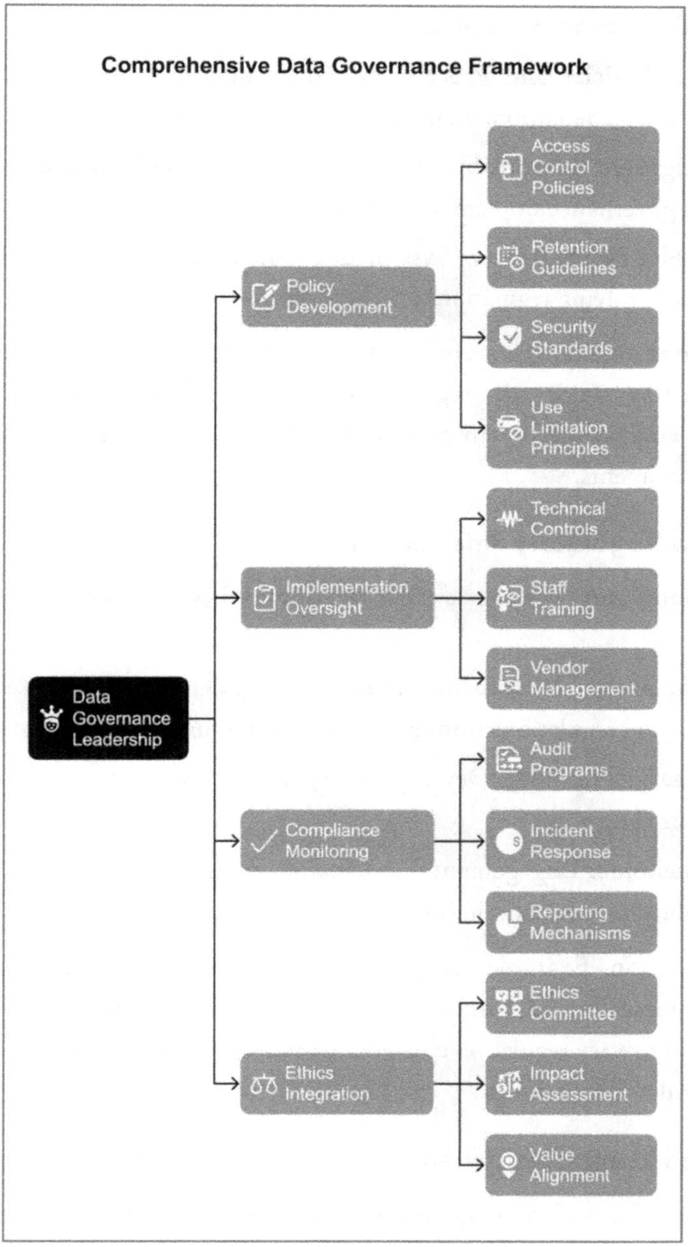

FIGURE 11.2: Comprehensive Data Governance Framework.

Essential Governance Components

- **Clear Policies and Procedures**: Establishing documented guidelines for data access, retention, security, and appropriate use
- **Designated Responsibility**: Appointing specific individuals accountable for data governance implementation and oversight
- **Regular Policy Review**: Systematically updating governance frameworks to reflect evolving regulations and best practices

Implementation Example: A healthcare network developed a comprehensive data governance framework including tiered access controls based on role necessity, data retention periods aligned with clinical and research needs, and regular third-party security assessments.

Proactive Regulatory Adaptation

Organizations can develop systematic approaches to managing regulatory evolution:

- **Continuous Monitoring Systems**: Implementing processes to track emerging regulations from proposal through implementation
- **Scenario Planning**: Developing responses to potential regulatory changes before they occur
- **Stakeholder Engagement**: Participating in regulatory development through public comment and industry associations

Implementation Example: A pharmaceutical company established a cross-functional regulatory adaptation team that regularly conducts scenario planning for potential privacy regulation changes, developing implementation roadmaps for various regulatory outcomes.

Enhanced Transparency and Patient Empowerment

Building on the patient engagement principles from Chapter 5, ethical data governance requires meaningful transparency:

- **Accessible Privacy Communications**: Creating clear, understandable explanations of data practices

- **Layered Information Presentation**: Providing both summary and detailed privacy information to accommodate different needs
- **Patient Control Mechanisms**: Implementing usable interfaces for managing privacy preferences

Implementation Example: A health system redesigned its privacy notices using plain language principles, consumer testing, and multiple formats (including video explanations) to ensure patients with different literacy levels and learning styles could understand their rights and options.

Patient Education and Empowerment

Ethical data practices require informed patients who understand their rights and options:

- **Multilevel Education Programs**: Providing information tailored to different knowledge levels and interests
- **Decision Support Tools**: Creating resources helping patients make informed choices about data sharing
- **Feedback Mechanisms**: Establishing channels for patients to express concerns and preferences

Implementation Example: A healthcare provider developed a digital privacy assistant that helps patients understand data sharing options, visualize which parties have access to their information, and adjust privacy settings through an intuitive interface.

Final Thoughts: The Future of Ethical EHR Utilization

As EHR systems continue the evolution described throughout this book, ethical considerations will become increasingly central to successful implementation. Several key trends will shape this landscape:

Patient-Centered Data Stewardship

The future of ethical EHR utilization will increasingly emphasize patient control and benefit:

- **Patient Data Ownership Models**: Technical frameworks giving individuals genuine authority over their health information
- **Community Data Governance**: Collaborative approaches involving patient communities in data stewardship decisions
- **Value Return Systems**: Models ensuring patients receive direct benefits from the use of their data

Algorithmic Ethics and Transparency

As AI becomes increasingly embedded in healthcare (Chapter 10), ethical implementation will require:

- **Algorithmic Fairness Standards**: Formal requirements for ensuring equitable performance across populations
- **Explainable AI Implementation**: Systems designed to provide understandable rationales for recommendations
- **Continuous Bias Monitoring**: Ongoing assessment for unexpected or emergent biases in real-world use

Global Ethical Frameworks

The international nature of healthcare data will necessitate:

- **Cross-Border Ethical Standards**: Harmonized approaches to data protection across jurisdictions
- **Cultural Competence in Ethics**: Recognition of varying values and priorities across populations
- **Inclusive Governance Models**: Ensuring diverse global representation in ethical framework development

Ethical Innovation Integration

Rather than viewing ethics as a constraint, forward-thinking organizations will:

- **Incorporate Ethics in Design Processes**: Building ethical consideration into the earliest stages of development
- **Measure Ethical Impact**: Assessing technology implementations on ethical dimensions alongside clinical and financial metrics
- **Cultivate Ethical Leadership**: Developing executives who prioritize ethical considerations in strategic decisions

The healthcare organizations that most effectively navigate these ethical dimensions—balancing innovation with responsibility, transparency with privacy, and progress with equity—will ultimately deliver the greatest value to patients, providers, and the broader healthcare ecosystem.

As we conclude our exploration of Electronic Health Records and their application in pharmaceutical marketing, this ethical framework provides the essential foundation. By grounding technological advancement in strong ethical principles, we can realize the full potential of healthcare data to improve outcomes while maintaining the trust that forms the core of the healthcare relationship.

Chapter Twelve

The Road Ahead What's Next for EHRs in Healthcare and Pharma

A New Era of Data-Driven Healthcare

Throughout this book, we have explored the evolution of Electronic Health Records from basic digital documentation systems to sophisticated platforms enabling targeted marketing, enhanced patient engagement, and improved clinical outcomes. As we conclude our journey, we turn our focus toward the horizon—examining how emerging technologies and changing healthcare paradigms will shape the future of EHRs and their application in pharmaceutical contexts.

The future of EHRs extends far beyond mere data collection. We stand at the threshold of an era where healthcare information systems will deliver actionable insights, enable unprecedented security models, and fundamentally empower patients as partners in their care. Building on the emerging technology foundations explored in Chapter 10 and the ethical frameworks established in Chapter 11, this final chapter examines how these developments will transform healthcare delivery and pharmaceutical engagement.

This chapter explores:

- The pivotal role of EHRs in advancing precision medicine initiatives
- Next-generation AI-driven clinical decision support and pharmaceutical applications
- How interoperability, blockchain, and real-world evidence will fundamentally reshape healthcare information systems
- Actionable strategies for healthcare organizations and pharmaceutical companies preparing for the next decade

Convergence of EHRs and Precision Medicine

As examined in Chapter 10, Electronic Health Records contain extraordinary potential for personalizing healthcare at both individual and population levels. The convergence of comprehensive patient data with advanced analytics creates unprecedented opportunities to tailor interventions based on specific patient characteristics.

Clinical Trial Transformation

Building on the pharmaceutical marketing strategies discussed in Chapters 7 and 8, EHR data will revolutionize clinical research through:

- **Precision Patient Identification**: Advanced algorithms analyzing EHR data can identify ideal candidates for specific clinical trials based on detailed phenotypic and genotypic characteristics
- **Protocol Optimization**: Historical EHR-derived outcomes data enables trial designs accounting for real-world variables often excluded from traditional studies
- **Synthetic Control Arms**: For rare conditions or when placebo controls are ethically problematic, EHR data can create robust comparison groups based on historical patients

Example: A pharmaceutical company developing a novel treatment for an aggressive subtype of inflammatory bowel disease leveraged EHR data to identify patients with specific genetic variants and inflammatory markers. This precision approach increased trial enrollment rates by 68% while reducing screen failures by 40%, accelerating development timelines by nearly a year.

Implementing the Precision Medicine Vision

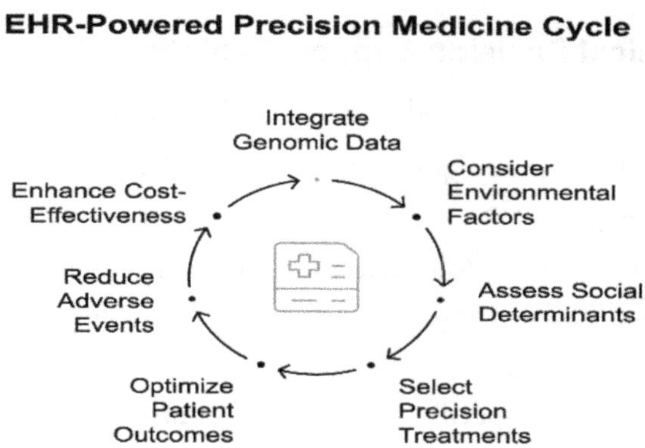

FIGURE 12.1: EHR-Powered Precision Medicine Model.

Personalized Therapeutic Approaches

The integration of comprehensive data sources within EHRs enables increasingly individualized treatment:

- **Pharmacogenomic Integration**: Combining genetic profiles with EHR data allows prediction of medication responses and adverse effect risks
- **Dynamic Dosing Optimization**: Continuous analysis of patient response data enables real-time dosage adjustments optimized for individual metabolic variations
- **Comorbidity-Aware Recommendations**: Algorithms considering multiple concurrent conditions can recommend treatment approaches minimizing cross-condition interactions

Example: An integrated health system implemented a precision medicine initiative incorporating genomic testing results directly into their EHR. When prescribing anticoagulants, clinicians received automated guidance on medication selection and dosing based on the patient's CYP2C9 and VKORC1 genotypes. This reduced adverse bleeding events by 27% and decreased hospitalizations related to suboptimal anticoagulation by 32%.

The Next Generation of AI-Driven Healthcare

While Chapter 10 introduced the foundations of AI in healthcare, the future holds much more sophisticated applications that will fundamentally transform both clinical practice and pharmaceutical engagement.

Advanced Clinical Decision Support Evolution

The next generation of AI-powered clinical decision support will feature:

- **Multimodal Data Integration**: Systems analyzing structured EHR data alongside imaging, genomics, and patient-generated information
- **Continuous Learning Algorithms**: Models that dynamically improve based on outcomes feedback and emerging medical evidence
- **Contextual Awareness**: AI that considers clinical setting, resource availability, and specific patient circumstances when generating recommendations

Example: A healthcare system deployed an advanced sepsis prediction model that continuously monitors patient data from multiple sources. Unlike earlier rule-based systems, this AI analyzes subtle patterns across laboratory values, vital signs, medication responses, and clinical documentation. The system identifies developing sepsis an average of 6 hours earlier than traditional methods, reducing mortality by 23% and ICU stays by 17%.

Pharmaceutical Applications of Advanced AI

Building on the marketing applications explored in Chapters 7 and 8, pharmaceutical companies will leverage next-generation AI for:

- **Treatment Response Prediction**: Models identifying which patients will likely respond to specific therapies
- **Real-World Comparative Effectiveness**: Systems analyzing treatment outcomes across diverse patient populations and practice settings
- **Adverse Event Pattern Recognition**: Algorithms detecting subtle safety signals across large patient populations

Implementation Considerations: As pharmaceutical organizations implement these advanced capabilities, they must carefully address the ethical considerations outlined in Chapter 11, particularly regarding algorithm transparency, bias prevention, and appropriate human oversight.

Case Study: How AI-Powered EHR Analytics Transformed Cancer Treatment

The Challenge: Overcoming One-Size-Fits-All Oncology Approaches

A leading cancer center faced challenges with standardized treatment protocols that produced variable outcomes. Despite access to cutting-edge therapies, oncologists lacked the ability to predict which patients would respond to specific regimens, leading to trial-and-error approaches that delayed effective intervention.

Strategic Solution: Comprehensive Data Integration and Predictive Modeling

The center implemented a sophisticated approach combining:

- **Multimodal Data Analysis**: Integration of comprehensive EHR data with genomic sequencing, proteomics, and advanced imaging
- **Machine Learning Treatment Matching**: Algorithms analyzing thousands of prior cases to identify patterns predicting treatment response
- **Continuous Learning System**: A dynamic model that improved recommendations as new outcome data became available

Measurable Outcomes

The initiative produced remarkable clinical improvements:

- 30% increase in first-line treatment effectiveness through personalized therapy selection
- Significant reduction in adverse effects by matching treatments to individual patient characteristics
- Accelerated treatment decision-making, particularly critical for aggressive cancer types

Key Implementation Insights

- EHR systems must evolve beyond documentation to become platforms for advanced analytics
- Predictive models require rigorous validation across diverse patient populations
- Effective implementation depends on clinician trust, requiring transparent AI recommendations with clear explanations

This case demonstrates how the future of EHRs extends far beyond the basic documentation and data exchange functions discussed in earlier chapters, becoming sophisticated platforms for knowledge generation and clinical decision optimization.

Interoperability Without Borders: The Connected Healthcare Ecosystem

While Chapter 2 examined current interoperability challenges, the future promises much more comprehensive solutions enabling truly connected healthcare.

Global Health Information Exchange

The evolution of interoperability standards will enable:

- **Cross-Border Patient Data Access**: Standardized protocols allowing authorized access to patient records regardless of geographic location
- **Universal Health Information Exchanges**: Networks connecting disparate systems through sophisticated translation and mapping capabilities
- **Patient-Centered Record Control**: Individuals managing a single comprehensive health record accessible to providers worldwide

Key Technology Enabler: The widespread adoption of FHIR (Fast Healthcare Interoperability Resources) standards, introduced in Chapter 2, will accelerate with next-generation implementation capabilities including:

- Dynamic mapping between legacy data formats and FHIR resources
- Standardized FHIR-based APIs for seamless third-party application integration
- Automated semantic harmonization of terminologies across systems

Blockchain-Secured Health Information

Building on the security concepts introduced in Chapter 3 and the blockchain technologies explored in Chapter 10, distributed ledger approaches will revolutionize health data management:

- **Patient-Controlled Access**: Cryptographic solutions giving individuals granular control over who accesses their information and for what purposes
- **Immutable Audit Trails**: Tamper-proof records of all data access and modifications ensuring transparency and accountability
- **Smart Contract Automation**: Self-executing agreements managing consent and data sharing without requiring intermediaries

Example Implementation: A regional health information exchange implemented a blockchain-based consent management system allowing patients to specify exactly which elements of their health record could be shared with specific provider types. The system automatically enforces these preferences while maintaining a comprehensive, tamper-proof audit trail of all data access. This increased patient participation in data sharing by 64% while reducing privacy complaints by 83%.

Remote Monitoring Integration and the Continuous Care Model

As introduced in Chapter 10, the integration of remote monitoring technologies with EHRs will enable a shift from episodic to continuous care:

The Connected Patient Ecosystem

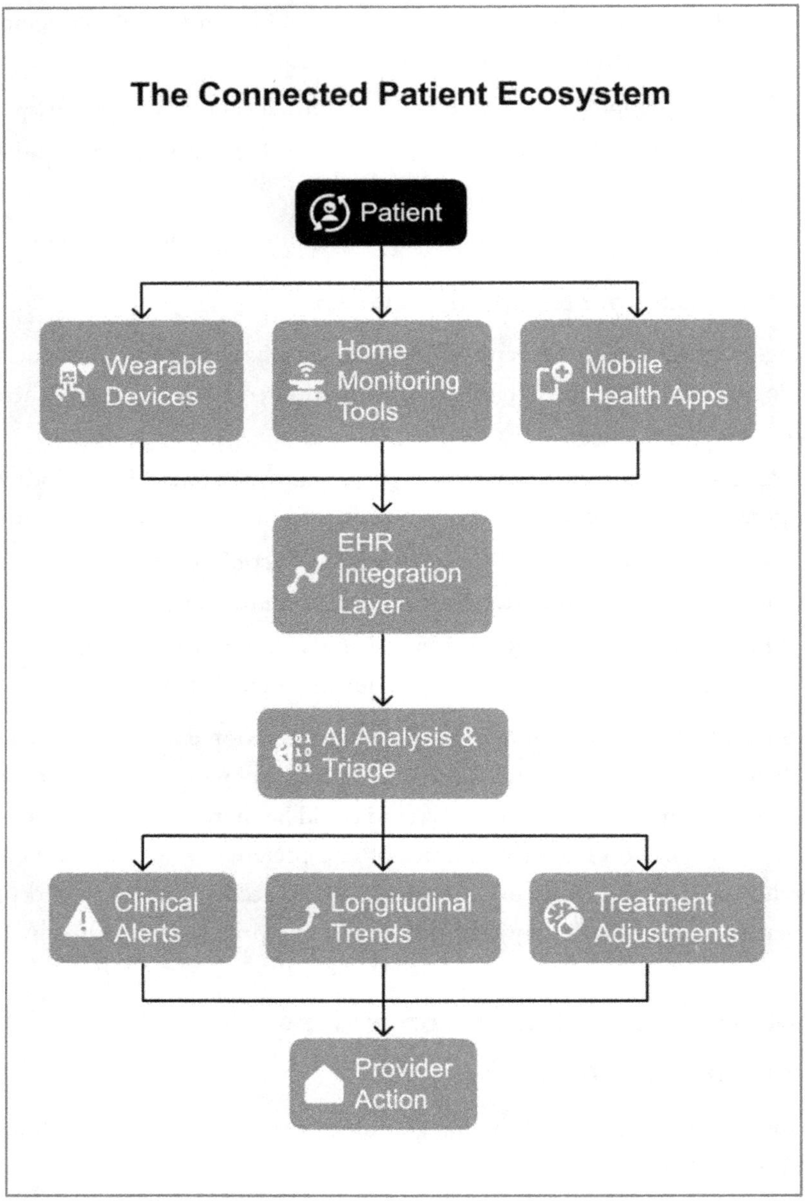

FIGURE 12.2: Integrated Remote Monitoring Ecosystem.

Pharmaceutical Applications of Connected Health

Building on the patient engagement strategies in Chapter 5, pharmaceutical companies will leverage connected health for:

- **Real-Time Adherence Monitoring**: Direct observation of medication utilization patterns
- **Therapeutic Effectiveness Assessment**: Continuous monitoring of clinical parameters indicating treatment response
- **Early Intervention Opportunities**: Identification of deterioration signals enabling proactive intervention

Example: A pharmaceutical company partnered with a digital health firm to develop a connected medication delivery system for patients with severe asthma. The smart inhaler tracked medication usage patterns and respiratory parameters, sending data directly to the patient's EHR. When the system detected deteriorating breathing patterns or suboptimal medication adherence, it triggered clinical outreach, reducing emergency department visits by 47% and improving quality of life scores by 38%.

Real-World Evidence: Transforming Drug Development and Evaluation

Building on the RWE concepts introduced in Chapter 11, EHR-derived real-world data will fundamentally reshape pharmaceutical research and regulatory processes:

The Evolution of Evidence Generation

Next-generation RWE approaches will include:

- **Hybrid Trial Designs**: Studies combining traditional randomized elements with real-world data collection
- **Pragmatic Clinical Trials**: Large-scale studies conducted within routine clinical care settings using EHR infrastructure
- **Continuous Post-Market Surveillance**: Ongoing monitoring of safety and effectiveness across entire patient populations

Key Enabler: Advanced data quality assessment methodologies will address the limitations of retrospective EHR data discussed in Chapter 11, enabling more confident regulatory and clinical decision-making based on real-world information.

Regulatory Pathway Transformation

Regulatory frameworks will evolve to incorporate RWE throughout the product lifecycle:

- **Accelerated Approval Pathways**: Conditional approvals based on surrogate endpoints with confirmatory evidence from RWE studies
- **Label Expansion Efficiency**: Streamlined processes for adding indications based on real-world usage patterns and outcomes
- **Synthetic Control Applications**: Use of historically matched patients from EHR data to augment or replace traditional control arms

Example: A regulatory agency approved a new indication for an existing oncology drug based primarily on a RWE study comparing outcomes in 12,000 patients who received the therapy off-label to matched controls from EHR systems. This approach reduced time to approval by approximately 2.5 years compared to a traditional randomized trial, making the therapy available sooner to patients with limited treatment options.

Preparing for the Next Decade: Strategic Imperatives

Healthcare organizations and pharmaceutical companies must take specific actions now to prepare for this rapidly evolving future:

For Healthcare Organizations

1. **Invest in Advanced Analytics Infrastructure**
    - Develop robust data lakes integrating clinical, financial, and operational information
    - Implement flexible analytics platforms supporting diverse modeling approaches
    - Create governance frameworks ensuring data quality and accessibility
2. **Prioritize Interoperability Implementation**
    - Adopt FHIR standards throughout all systems and interfaces
    - Participate in regional and national health information exchanges
    - Develop API strategies enabling innovation while maintaining security
3. **Establish Comprehensive Security Frameworks**
    - Implement zero-trust security architectures protecting data at all points
    - Deploy advanced identity and access management systems

- Create incident response capabilities addressing emerging threat vectors

4. **Build Data Science Capabilities**
   - Develop multidisciplinary teams combining clinical and analytical expertise
   - Establish continuous learning systems improving models based on outcomes
   - Create ethical review processes addressing AI-specific considerations

For Pharmaceutical Organizations

1. **Develop Real-World Data Strategies**
   - Create frameworks for evaluating and utilizing diverse real-world data sources
   - Establish partnerships with healthcare systems for ethical data access
   - Implement advanced analytics capabilities extracting value from unstructured information
2. **Transform Clinical Research Approaches**
   - Design protocol templates incorporating EHR-based recruitment and monitoring
   - Develop capabilities for running decentralized and hybrid clinical trials
   - Create infrastructure supporting synthetic control methodologies
3. **Enhance Patient Engagement Models**
   - Implement connected health platforms supporting continuous patient monitoring
   - Develop patient-centered applications improving therapeutic adherence
   - Create feedback mechanisms enabling patient-reported outcome collection
4. **Address Ethical and Regulatory Considerations**
   - Establish comprehensive governance for AI and advanced analytics
   - Develop transparent policies regarding data utilization and patient rights
   - Create proactive engagement with evolving regulatory frameworks

Implementation Readiness Assessment Framework

Capability Domain	Foundational Elements	Advanced Implementation	Leading-Edge Practice
Data Infra-structure	• Structured data repository • Basic interoperability • Standard security	• Integrated data lake • FHIR implementation • Advanced encryption	• Multi-source data integration • Seamless external exchange • Zero-trust architecture
AI & Analytics	• Retrospective analysis • Basic predictive models • Standard dashboards	• Near real-time analytics • Advanced prediction • Natural language processing	• Continuous learning systems • Multimodal AI integration • Ambient intelligence
Clinical Integration	• Basic decision support • Standard care pathways • Alert functionality	• Contextual recommendations • Personalized pathways • Risk stratification	• AI-augmented decisions • Precision medicine workflows • Autonomous monitoring
Patient Engagement	• Patient portals • Basic telehealth • Educational resources	• Connected health platforms • Remote monitoring • Digital therapeutics	• Continuous engagement • Predictive outreach • Fully integrated virtual care
Governance & Ethics	• Security compliance • Privacy policies • Standard oversight	• Data ethics frameworks • Algorithm validation • Transparency reporting	• Patient-controlled governance • Ongoing bias monitoring • Community oversight

FIGURE 12.3: Next-Generation EHR Implementation Readiness Framework.

Final Thoughts: The Future of EHRs and the Healthcare Revolution

As we conclude our exploration of Electronic Health Records and their application in pharmaceutical contexts, it's clear that we stand at the threshold of a fundamental transformation in healthcare. By 2035, EHRs will evolve from primarily documentation and communication systems to become active, intelligent participants in clinical decision-making and patient care.

The integration of artificial intelligence, blockchain technology, advanced interoperability, and real-world evidence capabilities will create a healthcare ecosystem that is:

- **Predictive rather than reactive**: Identifying and addressing health risks before they lead to significant illness
- **Personalized rather than standardized**: Tailoring interventions to individual characteristics rather than population averages
- **Continuous rather than episodic**: Monitoring and supporting health across settings and throughout life stages
- **Patient-directed rather than provider-controlled**: Empowering individuals as active partners in their health journey

For this vision to be realized, healthcare organizations, pharmaceutical companies, technology developers, and policy makers must collaborate closely, guided by the ethical principles outlined in Chapter 11. The challenge lies not merely in implementing new technologies, but in fundamentally redesigning care processes, business models, and patient relationships to leverage these capabilities effectively.

The next decade will determine how successfully we navigate this transformation—balancing innovation with responsibility, efficiency with empathy, and technological advancement with human connection. By thoughtfully applying the principles and strategies outlined throughout this book, organizations can help shape a future where Electronic Health Records serve as the foundation for healthcare that is simultaneously more precise, more personalized, and more humane.

Epilogue: The Next Chapter in Healthcare – A Look Into The Future

The Year 2035: A Glimpse into Tomorrow's Healthcare

As we reach the conclusion of our exploration of Electronic Health Records and their transformative potential, it is worth taking a moment to envision how the technologies, strategies, and ethical frameworks discussed throughout this book might converge to reshape healthcare in the coming decades.

It's the year 2035, and healthcare has undergone a transformation that extends far beyond the foundational changes described in Chapter 1 or the emerging technologies examined in Chapter 10. Hospitals have moved beyond the fragmented record systems and interoperability challenges outlined in Chapter 2. Instead, EHRs have evolved into fully integrated, AI-powered ecosystems that anticipate, diagnose, and manage care in real time. The blockchain security approaches introduced in Chapter 10 have become standard practice, ensuring privacy, security, and seamless global interoperability. The wearable technologies and remote monitoring systems discussed in Chapters 5 and 10 now continuously feed real-time health metrics into EHRs, enabling providers to deliver truly hyper-personalized treatment plans that address diseases before they progress.

This epilogue ventures beyond our current horizon to imagine the next chapter of healthcare's digital evolution—exploring how the technologies, strategies, and ethical considerations examined throughout this book might ultimately converge to create a fundamentally transformed healthcare experience.

A Patient's Journey in the Future Healthcare System
Meet Emily: A Preventive Care Success Story

Emily, a 42-year-old professional, awakens to an alert on her AI-powered health assistant. Her advanced wearable biosensor—far more sophisticated than the monitoring devices described in Chapter 10—has detected a subtle but concerning cardiovascular irregularity. Before she experiences any noticeable symptoms, her physician's AI-driven system has already analyzed this pattern against Emily's comprehensive health history, genetic profile, and similar cases, flagging her condition as high-risk.

Within minutes, Emily's physician receives an automated early warning report that synthesizes her continuous health data, genetic risk factors, environmental exposures, and lifestyle patterns. The report includes AI-generated differential diagnoses with probability rankings and personalized treatment options. Shortly after, Emily receives a notification for a virtual consultation where her provider reviews these insights and recommendations.

Unlike the fragmented care coordination described in Chapter 1, Emily's experience demonstrates the ultimate evolution of integrated healthcare. Instead of waiting weeks for an appointment and undergoing redundant testing as described in our historical case studies, her physician makes immediate medication adjustments and initiates a preventive intervention plan—all within hours of the initial alert. Through this early action based on predictive analytics, Emily avoids a potential cardiac event that traditional reactive healthcare would have missed.

This level of proactive, preventive healthcare represents the culmination of the technological trends and strategic approaches explored throughout this book—shifted fully from reactive treatment to predictive wellness management.

The Next 10 Years: Key Innovations in EHR Technology

Building on the emerging technologies discussed in Chapter 10 and expanding beyond the future vision presented in Chapter 12, several key innovations will reshape EHR capabilities over the next decade:

The Maturation of AI-Driven EHRs

The AI foundations described in Chapters 10 and 12 will evolve into more sophisticated systems:

- **Advanced Predictive Analytics**: Models will continuously analyze multimodal patient data streams to detect disease signatures months or years before clinical manifestation
- **Hyper-Personalized Decision Support**: AI systems will generate treatment pathways customized to a patient's unique genetic profile, microbiome composition, lifestyle factors, and environmental exposures
- **Ambient Clinical Intelligence**: Natural language processing and computer vision technologies will automatically document clinical encounters, eliminating manual data entry while extracting meaningful insights from provider-patient conversations

Blockchain-Enabled Patient Data Sovereignty

The blockchain security concepts introduced in Chapter 10 will evolve into comprehensive frameworks for patient data control:

- **Self-Sovereign Health Records**: Patients will exercise complete ownership of their medical records through cryptographic keys, granting and revoking specific provider access in real time
- **Smart Contract Governance**: Automated compliance engines will manage consent, data sharing agreements, and regulatory requirements through self-executing code
- **Distributed Data Verification**: Cross-institutional verification systems will ensure the accuracy and consistency of health information across global care networks

Genomic Medicine Integration

Expanding far beyond the precision medicine approaches discussed in Chapter 12:

- **Continuous Genomic Analysis**: EHRs will routinely incorporate whole genome sequencing alongside regular monitoring of gene expression changes and epigenetic modifications
- **Pharmacogenomic Precision**: Medications will be automatically selected and precisely dosed based on a patient's specific genetic variants affecting drug metabolism and response
- **Gene Therapy Tracking**: EHRs will monitor outcomes from increasingly common gene editing treatments, correlating genetic modifications with long-term health impacts

Frictionless Global Interoperability

Moving well beyond the interoperability challenges outlined in Chapter 2:

- **Universal Health Information Exchange**: Global data standards will enable instant, secure access to comprehensive patient records regardless of geographic location
- **Cross-Border Care Coordination**: AI-powered translation systems will eliminate language barriers in medical documentation, enabling seamless international provider collaboration
- **Semantic Interoperability**: Advanced natural language processing will automatically harmonize terminologies across different systems and care contexts

Immersive Care Delivery Integration

Building on the patient engagement strategies in Chapter 5:

- **Digital Therapeutic Integration**: EHRs will seamlessly incorporate prescribed digital therapeutics, monitoring adherence and outcomes while adjusting treatment parameters
- **Extended Reality Interfaces**: Augmented and virtual reality systems will provide intuitive visualization of complex health data for both providers and patients
- **Holographic Telemedicine**: Beyond video consultations, providers will interact with patients through photorealistic holographic representations, enhancing the remote care experience

The Ethical Imperatives of AI-Powered Healthcare

Building on the ethical frameworks presented in Chapter 11, the advancement of AI in healthcare introduces nuanced ethical considerations that must continue to evolve alongside technological capabilities.

Benefits Realized Through Ethical Implementation

1. **Enhanced Diagnostic Accuracy and Timeliness:** AI-powered EHRs will achieve diagnostic accuracy surpassing human capabilities in many domains, detecting subtle disease patterns before clinical manifestation. However, as explored in Chapter 11, these systems must be developed with diverse training data to prevent algorithmic bias.

2. **Workflow Optimization and Provider Well-Being:** By automating documentation and routine cognitive tasks, AI will alleviate the administrative burden that contributes to provider burnout. This automation, however, must be implemented in ways that enhance rather than diminish the human elements of care discussed throughout this book.
3. **Healthcare Democratization and Access:** AI-augmented care delivery can extend specialized expertise to underserved areas, reducing healthcare disparities. As emphasized in Chapter 11, equitable implementation requires intentional strategies to ensure these benefits reach all populations.

Ethical Challenges Requiring Ongoing Vigilance

1. **Comprehensive Bias Prevention:** As AI systems become increasingly autonomous, ensuring they don't perpetuate or amplify existing healthcare disparities becomes even more critical. Building on the ethical AI principles in Chapter 11, healthcare organizations must implement continuous bias monitoring systems that detect and mitigate both obvious and subtle forms of algorithmic discrimination.
2. **Evolving Data Rights Frameworks:** The patient autonomy principles discussed in Chapter 11 must evolve into comprehensive frameworks that address increasingly complex questions: How will patients meaningfully consent to AI analysis of their data when these systems become too complex to explain simply? What rights do patients have regarding AI-generated insights derived from their information?
3. **Maintaining Human Judgment and Relationship:** As AI capabilities advance, maintaining the appropriate balance between algorithmic efficiency and human discernment becomes increasingly important. Healthcare must preserve human judgment, empathy, and the therapeutic relationship even as AI handles more cognitive aspects of care.

The Balanced Path Forward

Building on the ethical frameworks established throughout this book, the responsible evolution of AI in healthcare requires:

- **Inclusive Development Processes**: Ensuring diverse stakeholders—including patients from various backgrounds—participate meaningfully in AI system design and governance

- **Transparency by Design**: Creating AI systems architected from the beginning for explainability, allowing both providers and patients to understand the rationale behind recommendations
- **Continuous Ethical Oversight**: Establishing governance structures that regularly assess AI systems for unexpected consequences, bias emergence, or mission drift

Final Reflections: Healthcare's Digital Horizon

By 2040, the Electronic Health Record will have transformed from the digital documentation system described in Chapter 1 into the intelligent foundation of global healthcare. The technological foundations, strategic approaches, and ethical frameworks explored throughout this book will converge to create a healthcare ecosystem characterized by:

- **Anticipatory Care**: Health systems that identify and address potential health issues before clinical symptoms appear
- **Patient-Centered Data Models**: Information architectures that place individuals at the center of their health data ecosystem with meaningful control
- **Borderless Health Information**: Care continuity that transcends geographic and institutional boundaries through universal interoperability
- **Augmented Clinical Intelligence**: Decision support that enhances rather than replaces the uniquely human elements of healthcare

As we conclude this exploration of Electronic Health Records and their transformative potential, the fundamental question remains: How do we harness these powerful technologies to enhance human connection and compassion rather than diminish them? The answer lies in the thoughtful application of the principles presented throughout this book—balancing innovation with responsibility, efficiency with humanity, and technological advancement with timeless healing relationships.

The future of healthcare will be shaped not simply by what technology can do, but by how we choose to implement it in service of human health and wellbeing. By embracing the potential of digital transformation while remaining anchored in healthcare's humanistic foundations, we can create a future where technology enhances rather than replaces the essential human connections at the heart of healing.

Glossary of Acronyms and Key Terms

ADR (Adverse Drug Reaction): An unwanted or harmful reaction experienced following the administration of a drug or combination of drugs.

AI (Artificial Intelligence): Computer systems able to perform tasks that normally require human intelligence, such as visual perception, speech recognition, decision-making, and translation between languages.

API (Application Programming Interface): A set of rules and protocols that allows different software applications to communicate with each other.

Ambient Clinical Intelligence: Technology that automatically documents clinical encounters using voice recognition and AI, reducing manual documentation burden for healthcare providers.

Blockchain: A distributed, immutable ledger technology that records transactions across many computers so that any involved record cannot be altered retroactively.

CDSS (Clinical Decision Support System): A health information technology system designed to provide clinicians with knowledge and patient-specific information to help inform decisions about patient care.

CMS (Centers for Medicare & Medicaid Services): The federal agency that administers Medicare, Medicaid, and the Children's Health Insurance Program.

CRM (Customer Relationship Management): A technology for managing an organization's relationships and interactions with customers and potential customers.

Data Lake: A centralized repository that allows storage of structured and unstructured data at any scale, enabling advanced analytics.

De-identification: The process of removing identifying information from patient data to protect privacy while allowing the data to be used for research, analysis, or other purposes.

Digital Therapeutics: Evidence-based therapeutic interventions driven by high-quality software programs to prevent, manage, or treat a medical disorder or disease.

EHR (Electronic Health Record): A digital version of a patient's paper chart that makes information available instantly and securely to authorized users.

EMR (Electronic Medical Record): A digital version of a patient's chart at a single healthcare organization, containing the patient's medical history, diagnoses, and treatments.

Federated Learning: A machine learning approach that trains algorithms across multiple decentralized devices or servers holding local data samples, without exchanging the data itself.

FHIR (Fast Healthcare Interoperability Resources): A standard describing data formats and elements and an API for exchanging electronic health records.

GDPR (General Data Protection Regulation): A regulation in EU law on data protection and privacy that applies to all individuals within the European Union and the European Economic Area.

HCP (Healthcare Provider): An individual or institution that provides preventive, curative, promotional, rehabilitative, or palliative healthcare services to individuals, families, or communities.

HIE (Health Information Exchange): The electronic movement of health-related information among organizations according to nationally recognized standards.

HIPAA (Health Insurance Portability and Accountability Act): A US law designed to provide privacy standards to protect patients' medical records and other health information.

HL7 (Health Level Seven): A set of international standards for transfer of clinical and administrative data between software applications used by various healthcare providers.

Interoperability: The ability of different information systems, devices and applications to access, exchange, integrate and cooperatively use data in a coordinated manner.

IoT (Internet of Things): The network of physical objects embedded with sensors, software, and other technologies for the purpose of connecting and exchanging data with other devices and systems over the internet.

Machine Learning: A type of artificial intelligence that enables computers to learn without being explicitly programmed, focusing on the development of programs that can access data and use it to learn for themselves.

NLP (Natural Language Processing): A field of artificial intelligence that gives computers the ability to understand text and spoken words in much the same way as human beings.

Patient Portal: A secure online website that gives patients convenient, 24-hour access to personal health information.

Pharmacogenomics: The study of how genes affect a person's response to drugs, combining pharmacology and genomics to develop effective, safe medications and doses tailored to a person's genetic makeup.

PHI (Protected Health Information): Any information about health status, provision of healthcare, or payment for healthcare that can be linked to a specific individual under HIPAA.

PGHD (Patient-Generated Health Data): Health-related data created, recorded, or gathered by or from patients, family members or caregivers to help address a health concern.

Precision Medicine: An approach to patient care that allows doctors to select treatments that are most likely to help patients based on a genetic understanding of their disease.

RCT (Randomized Controlled Trial): A type of scientific experiment that aims to reduce bias when testing a new treatment by randomly allocating subjects to two or more groups, treating them differently, and then comparing them.

RWD (Real-World Data): Data relating to patient health status and/or the delivery of healthcare routinely collected from a variety of sources.

RWE (Real-World Evidence): Clinical evidence regarding the usage and potential benefits or risks of a medical product derived from analysis of RWD.

SDOH (Social Determinants of Health): The conditions in which people are born, grow, live, work and age that affect health outcomes.

Smart Contract: Self-executing contracts with the terms of the agreement directly written into code that automatically execute actions when predetermined conditions are met.

Synthetic Control Arm: A patient cohort created using real-world data and advanced statistical methods to serve as a control group in clinical trials, potentially reducing the need for placebo groups.

Telehealth: The use of electronic information and telecommunications technologies to support long-distance clinical healthcare, patient and professional health-related education, and public health and administration.

Wearables: Electronic devices that can be worn as accessories, embedded in clothing, implanted in the user's body, or even tattooed on the skin to collect data about users' personal health and exercise.

Zero-Trust Security: A security concept centered on the belief that organizations should not automatically trust anything inside or outside their perimeters and must verify everything trying to connect to their systems before granting access.

www.ingramcontent.com/pod-product-compliance
Lightning Source LLC
Chambersburg PA
CBHW071223230926
51849CB00001B/18
* 9 7 8 9 3 4 9 5 6 2 6 5 3 *